DAILY BREAD

A Messianic One-Year Bible Reading Journal

5783 / 2022-2023

ARIEL MEDIA  ARIELMEDIA.SHOP

Hebrew Cover text:
(Standard Edition)

"Et lechem chukenu ten lanu ha-yom.
(Give us this day our daily bread)."

— Matthew 6:11

Daily Bread (5783 / 2022-2023):
A Messianic One-Year Bible Reading Journal

Copyright © 2012-2022 Lars Enarson & John Enarson

Design & Layout: John Enarson & Sybe de Vos.
Additional information is found in the Endnotes.

Eleventh Standard Edition 2022   ISBN   978-1-7356404-3-3
Fourth Women's Edition 2022   ISBN   978-1-7356404-4-0

Ariel Media
PO Box 94, Lake Mills, IA 50450, USA

Ariel Media is a ministry of the Watchman International
arielmedia.shop | thewatchman.org

To report a typo or to give feedback, please contact:
feedback@thewatchman.org

In case of loss, please return to:

_____

_____

_____

_____

As a reward: $ _____

~Introduction~

I t is a great blessing to have a daily, balanced diet from the Word of God, and to read through the entire Bible in a year. The Master said: "It is written: 'Man shall not live on bread alone, but on every word that proceeds out of the mouth of God'" (Matt. 4:4, Deut. 8:3). As disciples of Messiah, we need to study the Scriptures in a disciplined way. Therefore it is our great joy to publish *Daily Bread: A Messianic One-Year Bible Reading Journal*.

The Bible has come to us from the Jewish people. The one-year Bible reading plan in DAILY BREAD is unique in several ways: (1) it follows the same Jewish division of the Scriptures that Messiah and the Apostles were familiar with; (2) it takes you through a portion from each section every day; (3) it follows the same text portions that all of Israel studies each week; (4) it complements these with the rest of the biblical text; (5) it includes a generous amount of information about the Jewish calendar, the Feasts, and what has happened in the history of Israel on different days.

The Jewish division of the Hebrew Bible (OT) is the same as the one found in Luke 24:44. Every day, except Sabbaths and holidays (see below), DAILY BREAD takes you through:

- one portion from the Torah (the Five Books of Moses);
- one portion from the Prophets;
- one portion from the Writings;
- one portion from the Apostles (NT).

We have included an optional track of readings in parentheses for anyone who wishes to read through the Apostolic Scriptures (NT) twice a year. Those who wish to follow this optional track and study the Gospels with the Epistles every day, simply add the apostolic reading in parentheses ().

The weekly Torah portion is called the *parashah* and is read in every synagogue all over the world each Sabbath. The Apostles encouraged disciples who were not Jewish to follow the synagogue's Scripture readings (see Acts 15:21). The weekly Torah portion is divided into seven shorter *aliyot* (plural), which constitute the daily Torah reading in this Bible reading plan. On the Sabbath, the seventh *aliyah* is read, together with the accompanying portion from the Prophets, called the *haftarah* (see Luke 4:16). DAILY BREAD also adds suggested Messianic readings from the Apostles on Sabbaths and Holidays.

In the Jewish Bible, the books of the Prophets include: Joshua, Judges, Samuel I & II, and Kings I & II, followed by Isaiah, Jeremiah, Ezekiel, and the twelve shorter Prophets. (Note that the entire Book of Jonah is read on the Day of Atonement.) The Writings start with Psalms, followed by Proverbs, Job, and the five Scrolls which are read on special occasions: Song of Songs (Passover), Ruth (Feast of Weeks), Lamentations (9th of Av), Ecclesiastes (Tabernacles), and Esther (Purim). After these come: Daniel, Ezra, Nehemiah, and Chronicles I & II.

The composition of the Apostolic Scriptures (NT) is somewhat different in the East around the Land of Israel. In this earlier, Greek, manuscript tradition, the letters of Jacob (James), Peter, John, and Judah (Jude) follow directly after the Book of Acts. Paul writes in Galatians that "James, Cephas and John, those esteemed as pillars," were apostles before him in Jerusalem (Gal. 2:9, 1:17). Then come the letters of Paul, Hebrews, and the Book of Revelation.

We recommend reading all the daily Scripture portions early in the morning. If time does not allow, read the rest in the evening. Alternatively, you can read two portions in the morning and two in the evening. If you fall behind, you can catch up on the Sabbath, but a disciplined daily reading of the Word is best.

On each page in the journal you will find the Gregorian date, the Hebrew date, the Bible reading portions for the day, information about special events on the Hebrew calendar, and also the name of the Torah text for the week at the bottom of the page. Some days will have information about what happened in the Bible or in history on that specific day. On the empty lines, you can record what speaks to you from the Scriptures, prayer subjects, answers to prayer, etc.

We hope that you will be richly blessed by DAILY BREAD in your daily walk with the Master.

~ The Holy Books ~

Below are the books of Holy Scripture arranged according to the Jewish, Messianic tradition used in *Daily Bread*.

Torah

- Genesis
- Exodus
- Leviticus
- Numbers
- Deuteronomy

Prophets

- Joshua
- Judges
- Samuel I & II
- Kings I & II

- Isaiah
- Jeremiah
- Ezekiel
- The Twelve
  - I. Hosea
  - II. Joel
  - III. Amos
  - IV. Obadiah
  - V. Jonah
  - VI. Micah
  - VII. Nahum
  - VIII. Habakkuk
  - IX. Zephaniah
  - X. Haggai
  - XI. Zechariah
  - XII. Malachi

Writings

- Psalms
- Proverbs
- Job

- Song of Songs
- Ruth
- Lamentations
- Ecclesiastes
- Esther

- Daniel
- Ezra-Nehemiah
- Chronicles I & II

Apostles

- Matthew
- Mark
- Luke
- John

- Acts

- Jacob (James)
- 1 Peter
- 2 Peter
- 1 John
- 2 John
- 3 John
- Judah (Jude)

- Romans
- 1 Corinthians
- 2 Corinthians
- Galatians
- Ephesians
- Philippians
- Colossians
- 1 Thessalonians
- 2 Thessalonians
- 1 Timothy
- 2 Timothy
- Titus
- Philemon
- Hebrews

- Revelation

~The Biblical Year~

Below are the months and holy days of the biblical, Jewish calendar used in *Daily Bread*.

	MONTH	APROX. ROMAN	EVENTS
1	**NISAN**	Mar.–April	Passover, Unleavened Bread, First Fruits
2	**IYAR**	April–May	
3	**SIVAN**	May–June	Weeks (Pentecost)
4	**TAMUZ**	June–July	Fast of Tamuz
5	**AV**	July–Aug.	Fast of Av
6	**ELUL**	Aug.–Sep	
7	**TISHREI**	Sep.–Oct.	Trumpets, Fast of Gedaliah, Day of Atonement, Tabernacles
8	**CHESHVAN**	Oct.–Nov.	
9	**KISLEV**	Nov.–Dec.	Hanukkah
10	**TEVET**	Dec.–Jan.	Fast of Tevet
11	**SHVAT**	Jan.–Feb.	
12	**ADAR**	Feb.–Mar.	Fast of Ester, Purim
13	*Adar I*	*A leap-month added 7 years out of a 19-year cycle (years 3, 6, 8, 11, 14, 17, and 19)*	

Holy Days

DATE	EVENT	BIBLICAL REFERENCES
Nisan 14	PESACH (PASSOVER)	Ex. 12; Lev. 23:5; Num. 9:2f; 28:16; Dt 16:1f; Jos. 5:10; Eze. 45:21; Ezr. 6:19; 2 Chr. 30:1f; 35:17; Mt. 26:2f; Mk. 14:1f; Lk. 2:41; 22:1f; Jn. 2:13; 6:4; 11:55; 18:28f; 1 Cor. 5:7; Heb. 11:28
Nisan 15–21	CHAG HAMATZOT (UNLEAVENED BREAD)	Ex. 12:15f; 23:15; 34:18; Lev. 23:6; Num. 9:11; Dt. 16:3f; Jos. 5:11; Eze. 45:21; Ezra 6:22; 2 Chr. 8:13; 30:13f; 35:17; Mt. 26:17; Mk. 14:1; 14:12; Lk. 22:1f; Acts 12:3; 20:6; 1 Cor. 5:7
Nisan 16	BIKURIM/OMER (FIRST-FRUITS)	Lev. 23:9f; Mt. 28:1[1]; Acts 1:3[1]; 1 Cor. 15:20[1]
Sivan 6	SHAVUOT (WEEKS/PENTECOST)	Ex. 34:22; Lev. 23:15f; Num. 28:26; Dt. 16:10f; Ex. 19:16–20:21[1]; 2 Chr. 8:13; Acts 2:1f; 20:16; 1 Cor. 16:8
Tamuz 17[2]	TZOM TAMUZ (FAST OF TAMUZ)	Zec. 8:19; Ex. 32:6–35[1]
Av 9[2]	FAST OF AV (TISHA BE'AV)	Zec. 7:5; 8:19; Num. 14:28–30[1]; 2 Ki. 25:9; Lk. 19:41–44
Tishrei 1–2	ROSH HASHANAH (TRUMPETS)	Lev. 23:24; Num. 29:1; Zec. 9:14; Ezr. 3:6; Neh. 8:1; Mt. 24:31[1]; 1 Cor. 15:52[1]; 1 Thess. 4:16[1]; Rev. 11:15[1]
Tishrei 3[2]	TZOM GEDALIA (FAST OF GEDALIAH)	Zec. 7:3; 8:19; Jer. 41:2; 2 Ki. 25:25
Tishrei 10	YOM KIPPUR (DAY OF ATONEMENT)	Lev. 16; 23:27; Num. 29:7; Ex. 34:28–29[1]
Tishrei 15–21	SUKKOT (TABERNACLES)	Lev. 23:34f; Num. 29:12f; Dt. 16:13f; Zec. 14:16; Neh. 8:13; Jn. 7
Tishrei 22	SHMINI ATZERET (EIGHTH DAY)	Lev. 23:36; Num. 29:36f; 2 Chr. 7:9
Kislev 25–Tevet 2 or 3	HANUKKAH	Dan. 11; Jn. 10:22

Tevet 10[2]	**ASARA BETEVET** (FAST OF TEVET)	Zec. 8:19; Eze. 24:1f; 2 Ki. 25:1
Adar 13[2,3]	**TAANIT ESTER** (FAST OF ESTER)	Est. 4:16[1]; 9:1[1]
Adar 14[3]	**PURIM**	Est. 9:20–32
Adar 15[3]	**SHUSHAN PURIM** (PURIM IN JERUSALEM)	Est. 9:18–19

[1] Traditionally associated with the event.
[2] If this observance conflicts with Shabbat, the date of the event is moved.
[3] In a leap year, all events in Adar are held in Adar II.

~Blessings~

Torah studies (all Scripture included) is of even higher importance than prayer and should be done daily. Since it is a commandment (see Dt. 6:6–7) and a spiritual undertaking, it is customary in Israel to first pray and bless God before reading. These blessings are considered to cover all Scripture reading and studies for the rest of the day.

בָּרוּךְ אַתָּה יְיָ אֱלֹהֵינוּ מֶלֶךְ הָעוֹלָם, אֲשֶׁר קִדְּשָׁנוּ בְּמִצְוֹתָיו, וְצִוָּנוּ לַעֲסֹק בְּדִבְרֵי תוֹרָה. וְהַעֲרֶב נָא יְיָ אֱלֹהֵינוּ אֶת דִּבְרֵי תוֹרָתְךָ בְּפִינוּ, וּבְפִי עַמְּךָ בֵּית יִשְׂרָאֵל, וְנִהְיֶה אֲנַחְנוּ וְצֶאֱצָאֵינוּ, וְצֶאֱצָאֵי עַמְּךָ בֵּית יִשְׂרָאֵל, כֻּלָּנוּ יוֹדְעֵי שְׁמֶךָ, וְלוֹמְדֵי תוֹרָתְךָ לִשְׁמָהּ. בָּרוּךְ אַתָּה יְיָ, הַמְלַמֵּד תּוֹרָה לְעַמּוֹ יִשְׂרָאֵל.

Blessed are you, LORD our God, King of the universe, who has sanctified us with his commandments and has commanded us to engage in study of the words of Torah. Please, LORD our God, make the words of your Torah sweet in our mouth, and in the mouth of your people, the house of Israel. May we and our descendants, and the descendents of your people, the house of Israel, all know your name and study your Torah for its own sake. Blessed are you, LORD, who teaches Torah to his people Israel.

The Apostle Shaul Paul writes, "Then what advantage has the Jew? Or what is the benefit of circumcision? Great in every respect. First of all, they were entrusted with the oracles of God" (Rom. 3:1–2). Jews therefore pray:

בָּרוּךְ אַתָּה יְיָ אֱלֹהֵינוּ מֶלֶךְ הָעוֹלָם, אֲשֶׁר בָּחַר בָּנוּ מִכָּל הָעַמִּים, וְנָתַן לָנוּ אֶת תּוֹרָתוֹ. בָּרוּךְ אַתָּה יְיָ, נוֹתֵן הַתּוֹרָה.

Blessed are you, LORD our God, King of the universe, who has chosen us from all peoples and given us his Torah. Blessed are you, LORD, giver of the Torah.

For all believers in Messiah:

בָּרוּךְ אַתָּה יְיָ אֱלֹהֵינוּ מֶלֶךְ הָעוֹלָם, אֲשֶׁר נוֹתֵן תּוֹרַת אֱמֶת וּבְשׂוֹרַת יְשׁוּעָה לְעַמּוֹ יִשְׂרָאֵל וּלְכָל הָעַמִּים עַל־יְדֵי בְּנוֹ יֵשׁוּעַ הַמָּשִׁיחַ אֲדֹנֵינוּ.

Blessed are you, LORD our God, King of the universe, who gives the Torah of truth and the good news of salvation to his people Israel and to all peoples through his Son, Yeshua the Messiah, our Master.

18 Oct. / 23 Tishrei

TUESDAY
OUTSIDE ISRAEL: **SIMCHAT TORAH***
(REJOICING OF THE TORAH)

Deuteronomy 33:8–34:12	**TORAH** ☐
Genesis 1:1–2:3	
Joshua 1–2	**PROPHETS** ☐
Psalm 1–2	**WRITINGS** ☐
Matthew 1 (James 1)	**APOSTLES** ☐

TODAY IN HISTORY: King Solomon sends the people home after a 14-day celebration. "Then on the twenty-third day of the seventh month he sent the people to their tents, rejoicing and happy of heart because of the goodness that the LORD had shown to David and to Solomon and to His people Israel" (2 Chr. 7:10).   * It is customary among the Jewish people, since ancient times, to double the festival sabbath (*yom tov*) outside Israel.

BERESHEET (IN THE BEGINNING)

☐ **TORAH**	Genesis 2:4–19	
☐ **PROPHETS**	Joshua 3–4	
☐ **WRITINGS**	Psalm 3–4	
☐ **APOSTLES**	Matthew 2 (James 2)	

19 Oct. / 24 Tishrei
WEDNESDAY

TODAY IN HISTORY: Confession of sin in Israel. "Now on the twenty-fourth day of this month the sons of Israel assembled with fasting, in sackcloth and with dirt upon them" (Neh. 9:1f).

BERESHEET (IN THE BEGINNING)

20 Oct. / 25 Tishrei
THURSDAY

Genesis 2:20–3:21 **TORAH** ☐
Joshua 5–6 **PROPHETS** ☐
Psalm 5 **WRITINGS** ☐
Matthew 3 (James 3) **APOSTLES** ☐

BERESHEET (IN THE BEGINNING)

21 Oct. / 26 Tishrei

CANDLE LIGHTING TIMES: _____

_____ BERESHEET (IN THE BEGINNING)

22 Oct. / 27 Tishrei
SHABBAT

Genesis 4:19–6:8 **TORAH** ☐
Isaiah 42:5–43:10 **HAFTARAH** ☐
Romans 1:18–32 **APOSTLES** ☐

BERESHEET (IN THE BEGINNING)

☐ **TORAH**	Genesis 6:9–22	
☐ **PROPHETS**	Joshua 8	
☐ **WRITINGS**	Psalm 7	
☐ **APOSTLES**	Matthew 5 (James 5)	

23 Oct. / 28 Tishrei

SUNDAY

24 Oct. / 29 Tishrei
MONDAY

Genesis 7:1–16 **TORAH** ☐
Joshua 9 **PROPHETS** ☐
Psalm 8 **WRITINGS** ☐
Matthew 6 (1 Peter 1) **APOSTLES** ☐

NOACH (NOAH)

☐ **TORAH**	Genesis 7:17–8:14	
	Numbers 28:11–15	
☐ **PROPHETS**	Joshua 10	
☐ **WRITINGS**	Psalm 9	
☐ **APOSTLES**	Matthew 7 (1 Peter 2)	

25 Oct. / 30 Tishrei

● TUESDAY

ROSH CHODESH (DAY 1)

26 Oct. / 1 Cheshvan

WEDNESDAY ●
ROSH CHODESH (DAY 2)

Genesis 8:15–9:7   **TORAH** ☐
Numbers 28:11–15
Joshua 11–12   **PROPHETS** ☐
Psalm 10   **WRITINGS** ☐
Matthew 8 (1 Peter 3)   **APOSTLES** ☐

NOACH (NOAH)

☐ **TORAH**	Genesis 9:8–17	
☐ **PROPHETS**	Joshua 13	
☐ **WRITINGS**	Psalm 11–12	
☐ **APOSTLES**	Matthew 9 (1 Peter 4)	

27 Oct. / 2 Cheshvan
THURSDAY

28 Oct. / 3 Cheshvan
FRIDAY

Genesis 9:18–10:32 **TORAH** ☐
Joshua 14 **PROPHETS** ☐
Psalm 13–14 **WRITINGS** ☐
Matthew 10 (1 Peter 5) **APOSTLES** ☐

CANDLE LIGHTING TIMES:

NOACH (NOAH)

☐ **TORAH**   Genesis 11
☐ **HAFTARAH** Isaiah 54:1–55:5
☐ **APOSTLES** 2 Peter 3:1–14

29 Oct. / 4 Cheshvan
SHABBAT

30 Oct. / 5 Cheshvan
SUNDAY

Genesis 12:1–13   **TORAH** ☐
Joshua 15   **PROPHETS** ☐
Psalm 15–16   **WRITINGS** ☐
Matthew 11 (2 Peter 1)   **APOSTLES** ☐

TODAY IN HISTORY: Death of the "Bram," the Messianic pioneer Abram Poljak (zt"l) year 5724 (1963 CE). Poljak was a Ukranian-born, Orthodox Jew. A musical prodigy, he played violin for the Czar at the age of eight. As a young man, he moved to Germany and took work as a journalist. The writings of Leo Tolstoy brought him to faith in Yeshua. After a miraculous release from a Nazi prison, he immigrated to Israel after the war and contributed to the pioneering of the twentieth-century Messianic Jewish movement in Israel and abroad (vineofdavid.org).

LECH LECHA (GO FORTH)

31 Oct. / 6 Cheshvan
MONDAY

1 Nov. / 7 Cheshvan
TUESDAY ◑

Genesis 13:5–18 **TORAH** ☐
Joshua 18 **PROPHETS** ☐
Psalm 18 **WRITINGS** ☐
Matthew 13:1–30 (2 Peter 3) **APOSTLES** ☐

TODAY IN HISTORY: During the second Temple period, this was the time when the pilgrims who lived the farthest away (a 15-day journey) arrived home from Sukkot (Tabernacles) celebrations in Jerusalem (tradition).   In Israel prayers for rain are added to the liturgy (tradition).

LECH LECHA (GO FORTH)

□ **TORAH**   Genesis 14:1–20
□ **PROPHETS** Joshua 19–20
□ **WRITINGS** Psalm 19–20
□ **APOSTLES** Matthew 13:31–58 (1 John 1–2:11)

2 Nov. / 8 Cheshvan
WEDNESDAY

3 Nov. / 9 Cheshvan
THURSDAY

LECH LECHA (GO FORTH)

☐ **TORAH** Genesis 15:7–17:6
☐ **PROPHETS** Joshua 22
☐ **WRITINGS** Psalm 22
☐ **APOSTLES** Matthew 15 (1 John 3)

4 Nov. / 10 Cheshvan
FRIDAY

CANDLE LIGHTING TIMES: _____

_____

LECH LECHA (GO FORTH)

5 Nov. / 11 Cheshvan
SHABBAT

Genesis 17:7–27   **TORAH** ☐
Isaiah 40:27–41:16   **HAFTARAH** ☐
Romans 4:1–12   **APOSTLES** ☐

TODAY IN HISTORY: Death of Methuselah (tradition, Gen. 5:27). "So all the days of Methuselah were nine hundred and sixty-nine years, and he died." Death of Rachel (tradition, Gen. 35:18–20). "It came about as her soul was departing (for she died), that she named him Ben-oni; but his father called him Benjamin. So Rachel died and was buried on the way to Ephrath (that is, Bethlehem). Jacob set up a pillar over her grave; that is the pillar of Rachel's grave to this day."

LECH LECHA (GO FORTH)

☐ **TORAH**   Genesis 18:1–14
☐ **PROPHETS**   Joshua 23
☐ **WRITINGS**   Psalm 23–24
☐ **APOSTLES**   Matthew 16 (1 John 4)

6 Nov. / 12 Cheshvan
SUNDAY

7 Nov. / 13 Cheshvan
MONDAY

Genesis 18:15–33 **TORAH** ☐
Joshua 24 **PROPHETS** ☐
Psalm 25 **WRITINGS** ☐
Matthew 17 (1 John 5) **APOSTLES** ☐

VAYERA (AND HE APPEARED)

☐ **TORAH**	Genesis 19:1–20	
☐ **PROPHETS**	Judges 1	
☐ **WRITINGS**	Psalm 26	
☐ **APOSTLES**	Matthew 18 (2 John)	

8 Nov. / 14 Cheshvan

○ TUESDAY

9 Nov. / 15 Cheshvan
WEDNESDAY

Genesis 19:21–21:4   **TORAH** ☐
Judges 2   **PROPHETS** ☐
Psalm 27   **WRITINGS** ☐
Matthew 19 (3 John)   **APOSTLES** ☐

TODAY IN HISTORY: Jeroboam institutes an imitation festival in Israel (1 King. 12:27–33). "Jeroboam instituted a feast in the eighth month on the fifteenth day of the month, like the feast which is in Judah." Death of Matityahu the Maccabee (tradition, 1 Maccabees 2:70). "Then he blessed them, and was gathered to his ancestors. He died in the one hundred forty-sixth year and was buried in the tomb of his ancestors at Modein. And all Israel mourned for him with great lamentation" (NRSV). Kristallnacht (Night of Broken Glass), November 9, 1938.

VAYERA (AND HE APPEARED)

☐ **TORAH** Genesis 21:5–21
☐ **PROPHETS** Judges 3
☐ **WRITINGS** Psalm 28–29
☐ **APOSTLES** Matthew 20 (Judah (Jude))

10 Nov. / 16 Cheshvan
THURSDAY

11 Nov. / 17 Cheshvan
FRIDAY

Genesis 21:22–34   **TORAH** ☐
Judges 4   **PROPHETS** ☐
Psalm 30   **WRITINGS** ☐
Matthew 21 (Romans 1)   **APOSTLES** ☐

CANDLE LIGHTING TIMES:

TODAY IN HISTORY: The Great Flood begins (possible date, Gen. 7:11). "In the six hundredth year of Noah's life, in the second month [counting from Tishrei], on the seventeenth day of the month, on the same day all the fountains of the great deep burst open, and the floodgates of the sky were opened."

VAYERA (AND HE APPEARED)

13 Nov. / 19 Cheshvan
SUNDAY

Genesis 23:1–16   **TORAH** ☐
Judges 5   **PROPHETS** ☐
Psalm 31   **WRITINGS** ☐
Matthew 22 (Romans 2)   **APOSTLES** ☐

CHAYEI SARAH (SARA'S LIFE)

14 Nov. / 20 Cheshvan

MONDAY

CHAYEI SARAH (SARA'S LIFE)

15 Nov. / 21 Cheshvan
TUESDAY

Genesis 24:10–26   **TORAH** ☐
Judges 7   **PROPHETS** ☐
Psalm 33   **WRITINGS** ☐
Matthew 24:1–28 (Romans 4)   **APOSTLES** ☐

CHAYEI SARAH (SARA'S LIFE)

16 Nov. / 22 Cheshvan

◐ WEDNESDAY

17 Nov. / 23 Cheshvan
THURSDAY

Genesis 24:53–67   **TORAH** ☐
Judges 9   **PROPHETS** ☐
Psalm 35   **WRITINGS** ☐
Matthew 25 (Romans 6)   **APOSTLES** ☐

TODAY IN HISTORY: The Maccabees remove the defiled stones from the Temple (tradition, 1 Maccabees 4:43). Death of Messianic pioneer Rabbi Daniel Zion (z"l) year 5740 (1979 CE). Daniel Zion was one of the chief rabbis of Sofia, Bulgaria during World War II and believer in Messiah Yeshua. He was warned about the holocaust in a vision of the Master, and he helped save 800 Jews of Sofia from the Nazis but was himself interned in a concentration camp in 1943. In 1949 he emigrated to Israel (vineofdavid.org).

CHAYEI SARAH (SARA'S LIFE)

☐ **TORAH**	Genesis 25:1–11	
☐ **PROPHETS**	Judges 10–11	
☐ **WRITINGS**	Psalm 36	
☐ **APOSTLES**	Matthew 26:1–35 (Romans 7)	

18 Nov. / 24 Cheshvan

FRIDAY

CANDLE LIGHTING TIMES:

CHAYEI SARAH (SARA'S LIFE)

19 Nov. / 25 Cheshvan
SHABBAT

Genesis 25:12–18   **TORAH** ☐
1 Kings 1:1–31   **HAFTARAH** ☐
Galatians 4:21–31   **APOSTLES** ☐

CHAYEI SARAH (SARA'S LIFE)

☐ **TORAH**   Genesis 25:19–26:5
☐ **PROPHETS**   Judges 12–13
☐ **WRITINGS**   Psalm 37
☐ **APOSTLES**   Matthew 26:36–75 (Romans 8)

20 Nov. / 26 Cheshvan
SUNDAY

21 Nov. / 27 Cheshvan
MONDAY

Genesis 26:6–12   **TORAH** ☐
Judges 14–15   **PROPHETS** ☐
Psalm 38   **WRITINGS** ☐
Matthew 27:1–31 (Romans 9)   **APOSTLES** ☐

TODAY IN HISTORY: Noah leaves the ark (possible date, Gen 8:14f). "In the second month [counting from Tishrei], on the twenty-seventh day of the month, the earth was dry. Then God spoke to Noah, saying, 'Go out of the ark, you and your wife and your sons and your sons' wives with you.'"

TOLDOT (GENERATIONS)

☐ **TORAH** Genesis 26:13–22

☐ **PROPHETS** Judges 16

☐ **WRITINGS** Psalm 39

☐ **APOSTLES** Matthew 27:32–66 (Romans 10)

22 Nov. / 28 Cheshvan

TUESDAY

23 Nov. / 29 Cheshvan
WEDNESDAY

Genesis 26:23–29   **TORAH** ☐
Judges 17–18   **PROPHETS** ☐
Psalm 40   **WRITINGS** ☐
Matthew 28 (Romans 11)   **APOSTLES** ☐

TOLDOT (GENERATIONS)

24 Nov. / 30 Cheshvan

● THURSDAY
ROSH CHODESH

25 Nov. / 1 Kislev

FRIDAY ●
ROSH CHODESH

CANDLE LIGHTING TIMES:

TODAY IN HISTORY: The official start of winter in the Holy Land (tradition, *b.Bava Metzia* 106b).

TOLDOT (GENERATIONS)

27 Nov. / 3 Kislev
SUNDAY

Genesis 28:10–22   **TORAH** ☐
Judges 21   **PROPHETS** ☐
Psalm 44   **WRITINGS** ☐
Mark 3 (Romans 14)   **APOSTLES** ☐

VAYETZE (HE WENT OUT)

☐ **TORAH**	Genesis 29:1–17
☐ **PROPHETS**	1 Samuel 1
☐ **WRITINGS**	Psalm 45
☐ **APOSTLES**	Mark 4 (Romans 15)

28 Nov. / 4 Kislev
MONDAY

TODAY IN HISTORY: Zechariah recieves a prophecy about 'true' fasting (Zec. 7:1–14). In the fourth year of King Darius, the word of the LORD came to Zechariah on the fourth day of the ninth month, the month of Kislev" (NIV).

VAYETZE (HE WENT OUT)

29 Nov. / 5 Kislev
TUESDAY

VAYETZE (HE WENT OUT)

☐ **TORAH**	Genesis 30:14–27
☐ **PROPHETS**	1 Samuel 3
☐ **WRITINGS**	Psalm 48
☐ **APOSTLES**	Mark 6:1–29 (1 Corinthians 1)

30 Nov. / 6 Kislev

◐ WEDNESDAY

1 Dec. / 7 Kislev
THURSDAY

☐ **TORAH**	Genesis 31:17–42	
☐ **PROPHETS**	1 Samuel 6–7	
☐ **WRITINGS**	Psalm 50	
☐ **APOSTLES**	Mark 7 (1 Corinthians 3)	

2 Dec. / 8 Kislev
FRIDAY

CANDLE LIGHTING TIMES:

VAYETZE (HE WENT OUT)

3 Dec. / 9 Kislev
SHABBAT

VAYETZE (HE WENT OUT)

4 Dec. / 10 Kislev
SUNDAY

5 Dec. / 11 Kislev
MONDAY

Genesis 32:13–29[14–30]   **TORAH** ☐
1 Samuel 10–11   **PROPHETS** ☐
Psalm 52–53   **WRITINGS** ☐
Mark 9:1–29 (1 Corinthians 5)   **APOSTLES** ☐

VAYISHLACH (HE SENT)

□ **TORAH** Genesis 32:30[31]–33:5
□ **PROPHETS** 1 Samuel 12–13
□ **WRITINGS** Psalm 54–55
□ **APOSTLES** Mark 9:30–50 (1 Corinthians 6)

6 Dec. / 12 Kislev
TUESDAY

7 Dec. / 13 Kislev
WEDNESDAY

Genesis 33:6–20 **TORAH** ☐
1 Samuel 14 **PROPHETS** ☐
Psalm 56–57 **WRITINGS** ☐
Mark 10:1–31 (1 Corinthians 7:1–24) **APOSTLES** ☐

TODAY IN HISTORY: Birth of Reuben (tradition, Gen. 29:32). "Leah conceived and bore a son and named him Reuben, for she said, 'Because the LORD has seen my affliction; surely now my husband will love me.'"

VAYISHLACH (HE SENT)

9 Dec. / 15 Kislev
FRIDAY

Genesis 35:12–36:19 **TORAH** ☐
1 Samuel 17 **PROPHETS** ☐
Psalm 60–61 **WRITINGS** ☐
Mark 11 (1 Corinthians 8) **APOSTLES** ☐

CANDLE LIGHTING TIMES:

VAYISHLACH (HE SENT)

11 Dec. / 17 Kislev
SUNDAY

Genesis 37:1–11   **TORAH** ☐
1 Samuel 18   **PROPHETS** ☐
Psalm 62–63   **WRITINGS** ☐
Mark 12 (1 Corinthians 9)   **APOSTLES** ☐

VAYESHEV (HE SETTLED)

☐ **TORAH**   Genesis 37:12–22
☐ **PROPHETS**   1 Samuel 19
☐ **WRITINGS**   Psalm 64–65
☐ **APOSTLES**   Mark 13 (1 Corinthians 10)

12 Dec. / 18 Kislev
MONDAY

13 Dec. / 19 Kislev
TUESDAY

VAYESHEV (HE SETTLED)

□ **TORAH** Genesis 38
□ **PROPHETS** 1 Samuel 21–22
□ **WRITINGS** Psalm 68
□ **APOSTLES** Mark 14:43–72 (1 Corinthians 12)

14 Dec. / 20 Kislev
WEDNESDAY

TODAY IN HISTORY: Ezra the Scribe addresses the people (Ezr. 10:9–15). "So all the men of Judah and Benjamin assembled at Jerusalem within the three days. It was the ninth month on the twentieth of the month."

VAYESHEV (HE SETTLED)

15 Dec. / 21 Kislev
THURSDAY

VAYESHEV (HE SETTLED)

☐ **TORAH** Genesis 39:7–23
☐ **PROPHETS** 1 Samuel 25
☐ **WRITINGS** Psalm 70–71
☐ **APOSTLES** Mark 16 (1 Corinthians 14:1–19)

16 Dec. / 22 Kislev

◗ FRIDAY

CANDLE LIGHTING TIMES:

VAYESHEV (HE SETTLED)

17 Dec. / 23 Kislev
SHABBAT

Genesis 40   **TORAH** ☐
Amos 2:6–3:8   **HAFTARAH** ☐
John 19:14–24   **APOSTLES** ☐

VAYESHEV (HE SETTLED)

☐ **TORAH** Genesis 41:1–14
☐ **PROPHETS** 1 Samuel 26–27
☐ **WRITINGS** Psalm 72
☐ **APOSTLES** Luke 1:1–38 (1 Corinthians 14:20–40)

18 Dec. / 24 Kislev
SUNDAY
HANUKKAH EVE

TODAY IN HISTORY: Haggai receives prophecy for Israel and Zerubbabel (Hag. 2:10,18). "On the twenty-fourth of the ninth [month], in the second year of Darius, the word of the LORD came to Haggai the prophet… 'Do consider from this day onward, from the twenty-fourth day of the ninth month; from the day when the temple of the LORD was founded, consider.'"

MIKETZ (AT THE END)

19 Dec. / 25 Kislev

MONDAY
HANUKKAH DAY 1

Genesis 41:15–38	**TORAH** ☐
Numbers 7:1–17	
1 Samuel 28–29	**PROPHETS** ☐
Psalm 73	**WRITINGS** ☐
Luke 1:39–80 (1 Corinthians 15:1–28)	**APOSTLES** ☐

TODAY IN HISTORY: The Maccabees liberate the Temple (1 Maccabees 4). "…the twenty-fifth day of the ninth month, which is the month of Chislev…At the very season and on the very day that the Gentiles had profaned it, it was dedicated with songs and harps and lutes and cymbals" (NRSV). Messiah is at the Temple during Chanukah (possible date, Jn. 10:22f). "At that time the Feast of the Dedication took place at Jerusalem; it was winter, and Yeshua was walking in the temple in the portico of Solomon."

Suggested Historical Reading: First Book of Maccabees 1–2

MIKETZ (AT THE END)

Suggested Historical Reading: First Book of Maccabees 3–4

MIKETZ (AT THE END)

21 Dec. / 27 Kislev
WEDNESDAY
HANUKKAH DAY 3

Genesis 41:53–42:18   **TORAH** ☐
Numbers 7:24–35
2 Samuel 1   **PROPHETS** ☐
Psalm 75–76   **WRITINGS** ☐
Luke 2:22–52 (1 Corinthians 16)   **APOSTLES** ☐

Suggested Historical Reading: First Book of Maccabees 5–6

MIKETZ (AT THE END)

☐ **TORAH**	Genesis 42:19–43:15	
	Numbers 7:30–41	
☐ **PROPHETS**	2 Samuel 2	
☐ **WRITINGS**	Psalm 77	
☐ **APOSTLES**	Luke 3 (2 Corinthians 1)	

22 Dec. / 28 Kislev

TODAY IN HISTORY: Possible date of Gabriel's visit to Miriam in Nazareth, nine months before *Rosh HaShanah* and the fall feasts in the seventh month (Lk. 1:26–38).

Suggested Historical Reading: First Book of Maccabees 7–8

MIKETZ (AT THE END)

23 Dec. / 29 Kislev

FRIDAY
HANUKKAH DAY 5

Genesis 43:16–29   **TORAH** ☐
Numbers 7:36–47
2 Samuel 3   **PROPHETS** ☐
Psalm 78:1–39   **WRITINGS** ☐
Luke 4 (2 Corinthians 2)   **APOSTLES** ☐

CANDLE LIGHTING TIMES: ....

Suggested Historical Reading: First Book of Maccabees 9–10

MIKETZ (AT THE END)

☐ **TORAH**	Genesis 43:30–44:17
	Numbers 28:9–15; 7:42–47
☐ **HAFTARAH**	Zechariah 3:1[2:14]–4:7
☐ **APOSTLES**	Philippians 2:1–11

24 Dec. / 30 Kislev

● **SHABBAT**
ROSH CHODESH (DAY 1)
HANUKKAH DAY 6

Suggested Historical Reading: First Book of Maccabees 11–12

25 Dec. / 1 Tevet

SUNDAY ●

ROSH CHODESH (DAY 2)
HANUKKAH DAY 7

Genesis 44:18–30
Numbers 28:11–15; 7:48–53 **TORAH** ☐

2 Samuel 4–5 **PROPHETS** ☐
Psalm 78:40–72 **WRITINGS** ☐
Luke 5 (2 Corinthians 3) **APOSTLES** ☐

TODAY IN HISTORY: Ezra investigates the matter of foreign wives among Israel (Ezr. 10:16). "So they convened on the first day of the tenth month to investigate the matter." Esther is made queen (Est. 2:16–17). "So Esther was taken to King Ahasuerus to his royal palace in the tenth month which is the month Tebeth, in the seventh year of his reign."

Suggested Historical Reading: First Book of Maccabees 13–14

VAYIGASH (HE DREW NEAR)

☐ **TORAH**   Genesis 44:31–45:7
             Numbers 7:54–8:4
☐ **PROPHETS**   2 Samuel 6–7
☐ **WRITINGS**   Psalm 79–80
☐ **APOSTLES**   Luke 6:1–26 (2 Corinthians 4)

Suggested Historical Reading: First Book of Maccabees 15–16

VAYIGASH (HE DREW NEAR)

27 Dec. / 3 Tevet

TUESDAY

Genesis 45:8–18   **TORAH** ☐

2 Samuel 8–9   **PROPHETS** ☐

Psalm 81   **WRITINGS** ☐

Luke 6:27–49 (2 Corinthians 5)   **APOSTLES** ☐

☐ **TORAH** Genesis 45:19–27
☐ **PROPHETS** 2 Samuel 10–11
☐ **WRITINGS** Psalm 82–83
☐ **APOSTLES** Luke 7 (2 Corinthians 6)

28 Dec. / 4 Tevet
WEDNESDAY

29 Dec. / 5 Tevet
THURSDAY

TODAY IN HISTORY: The Prophet Ezekiel receives a report in Babylon. "Now in the twelfth year of our exile, on the fifth of the tenth month, the refugees from Jerusalem came to me, saying, 'The city has been taken.' (Eze. 33:21).

VAYIGASH (HE DREW NEAR)

☐ **TORAH**   Genesis 46:28–47:10
☐ **PROPHETS**   2 Samuel 13
☐ **WRITINGS**   Psalm 85
☐ **APOSTLES**   Luke 8:26–56 (2 Corinthians 8)

30 Dec. / 6 Tevet

◑ FRIDAY

CANDLE LIGHTING TIMES:

VAYIGASH (HE DREW NEAR)

31 Dec. / 7 Tevet
SHABBAT

Genesis 47:11–27   **TORAH** ☐
Ezekiel 37:15–28   **HAFTARAH** ☐
Acts 3:11–26   **APOSTLES** ☐

VAYIGASH (HE DREW NEAR)

1 Jan. / 8 Tevet
SUNDAY

TODAY IN HISTORY: 72 Jewish scholars complete the Greek translation of the Torah on behalf of the Greco-Egyptian king Ptolemy II. The translation is later called the Septuagint which means "seventy" (tradition, 246 BCE).

VAYECHI (HE LIVED)

2 Jan. / 9 Tevet
MONDAY

TODAY IN HISTORY: The martyrdom of the Apostle Shimon Peter (Kefa) bar Yonah (rabbinic tradition, *Megillat Ta'anit*, *Orach Chaim* 580). Christian traditions agree that he was crucified in Rome during the reign of Nero in 3825 (64 CE). "Truly, truly I tell you, when you were younger, you used to put on your belt and walk wherever you wanted; but when you grow old, you will stretch out your hands and someone else will put your belt on you, and bring you where you do not want to go.' Now He said this, indicating by what kind of death he would glorify God" (Jn 21:18–19). Death of Ezra the Scribe (tradition).

VAYECHI (HE LIVED)

☐ **TORAH**   Genesis 48:17–22

☐ **PROPHETS** 2 Samuel 16

☐ **WRITINGS** Psalm 88

☐ **APOSTLES** Luke 10 (2 Corinthians 11)

☐ **SYNAGOGUE READINGS**

Exodus 32:11–14; 34:1–10; Isaiah 55:6–56:8 (afternoon)

TODAY IN HISTORY: Nebuchadnezzar begins the siege of Jerusalem (2 Ki. 25:1). "Now in the ninth year of his reign, on the tenth day of the tenth month, Nebuchadnezzar king of Babylon came, he and all his army, against Jerusalem, camped against it and built a siege wall all around it." In Babylon, God tells Ezekiel of Jerusalem's siege 880 miles (1416 km) away (Eze. 24). "And the word of the LORD came to me in the ninth year, in the tenth month, on the tenth of the month, saying, 'Son of man, write the name of the day, this very day. The king of Babylon has laid siege to Jerusalem this very day.'" "Esther was taken to King Ahasuerus to his royal palace in the tenth month which is the month [Tevet], in the seventh year of his reign" (Est. 2:16). The fast of the tenth month (Zec. 8:19). The Fast of Tevet (*Asara BeTevet*) is a shorter fast on the Jewish calendar and lasts from sunrise to sunset. It is one of four similar, biblical fast days and commemorates the siege and destruction of Jerusalem and the Temple. It has no connection to Chanukah despite the fact that it occurs only a week after it.

VAYECHI (HE LIVED)

4 Jan. / 11 Tevet
WEDNESDAY

Genesis 49:1–18 **TORAH** ☐
2 Samuel 17 **PROPHETS** ☐
Psalm 89 **WRITINGS** ☐
Luke 11:1–28 (2 Corinthians 12) **APOSTLES** ☐

VAYECHI (HE LIVED)

5 Jan. / 12 Tevet

THURSDAY

TODAY IN HISTORY: The Prophet Ezekiel receives one in a series of seven prophecies (nearly all dated) against Egypt (Eze. 29–32). "In the tenth year, in the tenth month, on the twelfth of the month, the word of the LORD came to me saying, 'Son of man, set your face against Pharaoh king of Egypt and prophesy against him and against all Egypt.'"

VAYECHI (HE LIVED)

6 Jan. / 13 Tevet
FRIDAY

Genesis 49:27–50:20   **TORAH** ☐
2 Samuel 19   **PROPHETS** ☐
Psalm 91   **WRITINGS** ☐
Luke 12:1–34 (Galatians 1)   **APOSTLES** ☐

CANDLE LIGHTING TIMES:

VAYECHI (HE LIVED)

VAYECHI (HE LIVED)

8 Jan. / 15 Tevet
SUNDAY

SHMOT (NAMES)

☐ **TORAH**	Exodus 1:18–2:10	
☐ **PROPHETS**	2 Samuel 21	
☐ **WRITINGS**	Psalm 94	
☐ **APOSTLES**	Luke 13 (Galatians 3)	

9 Jan. / 16 Tevet
MONDAY

10 Jan. / 17 Tevet
TUESDAY

Exodus 2:11–25 **TORAH** ☐
2 Samuel 22 **PROPHETS** ☐
Psalm 95–96 **WRITINGS** ☐
Luke 14 (Galatians 4) **APOSTLES** ☐

SHMOT (NAMES)

☐ **TORAH** Exodus 3:1–15
☐ **PROPHETS** 2 Samuel 23
☐ **WRITINGS** Psalm 97–98
☐ **APOSTLES** Luke 15 (Galatians 5)

11 Jan. / 18 Tevet
WEDNESDAY

12 Jan. / 19 Tevet
THURSDAY

SHMOT (NAMES)

13 Jan. / 20 Tevet
FRIDAY

CANDLE LIGHTING TIMES: _____

SHMOT (NAMES)

14 Jan. / 21 Tevet
SHABBAT

Exodus 5:1–6:1 **TORAH** ☐
Jeremiah 1:1–2:3 **HAFTARAH** ☐
Acts 7:17–37 **APOSTLES** ☐

TODAY IN HISTORY: Birth of Simeon (tradition, Gen. 29:33). "Then she conceived again and bore a son and said, 'Because the LORD has heard that I am unloved, He has therefore given me this son also.' So she named him Simeon."

SHMOT (NAMES)

□ **TORAH** Exodus 6:2–13
□ **PROPHETS** 1 Kings 2
□ **WRITINGS** Psalm 103
□ **APOSTLES** Luke 18 (Ephesians 2)

15 Jan. / 22 Tevet
◐ SUNDAY

16 Jan. / 23 Tevet
MONDAY

Exodus 6:14–28 **TORAH** ☐
1 Kings 3–4 **PROPHETS** ☐
Psalm 104 **WRITINGS** ☐
Luke 19:1–27 (Ephesians 3) **APOSTLES** ☐

VA'ERA (I APPEARED)

☐ **TORAH**   Exodus 6:29–7:7
☐ **PROPHETS**   1 Kings 5–6
☐ **WRITINGS**   Psalm 105
☐ **APOSTLES**   Luke 19:28–48 (Ephesians 4)

17 Jan. / 24 Tevet
TUESDAY

18 Jan. / 25 Tevet
WEDNESDAY

Exodus 7:8–8:10[6] **TORAH** ☐
1 Kings 7 **PROPHETS** ☐
Psalm 106 **WRITINGS** ☐
Luke 20:1–26 (Ephesians 5) **APOSTLES** ☐

VA'ERA (I APPEARED)

☐ **TORAH**	Exodus 8:11–22[7–18]
☐ **PROPHETS**	1 Kings 8
☐ **WRITINGS**	Psalm 107
☐ **APOSTLES**	Luke 20:27–47 (Ephesians 6)

19 Jan. / 26 Tevet
THURSDAY

20 Jan. / 27 Tevet
FRIDAY

Exodus 8:23[19]–9:16   **TORAH** ☐

1 Kings 9   **PROPHETS** ☐

Psalm 108   **WRITINGS** ☐

Luke 21 (Philippians 1)   **APOSTLES** ☐

CANDLE LIGHTING TIMES:

VA'ERA (I APPEARED)

TODAY IN HISTORY: Death of Simeon (tradition, Ex. 1:6). "Joseph died, and all his brothers and all that generation."

22 Jan. / 29 Tevet
SUNDAY

Exodus 10:1–11   **TORAH** ☐
1 Kings 10   **PROPHETS** ☐
Psalm 109 –110   **WRITINGS** ☐
Luke 22:1–38 (Philippians 2)   **APOSTLES** ☐

TODAY IN HISTORY: The official end of winter in the Holy Land (tradition, *b.Bava Metzia* 106b).

BO (COME)

☐ **TORAH**	Exodus 10:12–23
	Numbers 28:11–15
☐ **PROPHETS**	1 Kings 11
☐ **WRITINGS**	Psalm 111–112
☐ **APOSTLES**	Luke 22:39–71 (Philippians 3)

23 Jan. / 1 Shvat
● MONDAY
ROSH CHODESH

BO (COME)

24 Jan. / 2 Shvat
TUESDAY

Exodus 10:24–11:3 **TORAH** ☐
1 Kings 12 **PROPHETS** ☐
Psalm 113–114 **WRITINGS** ☐
Luke 23:1–25 (Philippians 4) **APOSTLES** ☐

BO (COME)

☐ **TORAH**   Exodus 11:4–12:20
☐ **PROPHETS**   1 Kings 13
☐ **WRITINGS**   Psalm 115
☐ **APOSTLES**   Luke 23:26–56 (Colossians 1)

25 Jan. / 3 Shvat
WEDNESDAY

26 Jan. / 4 Shvat
THURSDAY

BO (COME)

☐ **TORAH**	Exodus 12:29–51	
☐ **PROPHETS**	1 Kings 15	
☐ **WRITINGS**	Psalm 118	
☐ **APOSTLES**	Luke 24:28–53 (Colossians 3)	

27 Jan. / 5 Shvat
FRIDAY

CANDLE LIGHTING TIMES:

BO (COME)

28 Jan. / 6 Shvat
SHABBAT ◑

Exodus 13:1–16   **TORAH** ☐
Jeremiah 46:13–28 **HAFTARAH** ☐
Revelation 16:1–21 **APOSTLES** ☐

BO (COME)

☐ **TORAH** Exodus 13:17–14:8
☐ **PROPHETS** 1 Kings 16
☐ **WRITINGS** Psalm 119:1–24
☐ **APOSTLES** John 1:1–28 (Colossians 4)

29 Jan. / 7 Shvat
SUNDAY

30 Jan. / 8 Shvat
MONDAY

Exodus 14:9–14 **TORAH** ☐
1 Kings 17 **PROPHETS** ☐
Psalm 119:25–48 **WRITINGS** ☐
John 1:29–51 (1 Thessalonians 1) **APOSTLES** ☐

BESHALACH (WHEN HE SENT)

□ **TORAH** Exodus 14:15–25
□ **PROPHETS** 1 Kings 18
□ **WRITINGS** Psalm 119:49–72
□ **APOSTLES** John 2 (1 Thessalonians 2)

31 Jan. / 9 Shvat
TUESDAY

1 Feb. / 10 Shvat
WEDNESDAY

Exodus 14:26–15:26 **TORAH** ☐
1 Kings 19 **PROPHETS** ☐
Psalm 119:73–96 **WRITINGS** ☐
John 3 (1 Thessalonians 3) **APOSTLES** ☐

BESHALACH (WHEN HE SENT)

3 Feb. / 12 Shvat
FRIDAY

Exodus 16:11–36   **TORAH** ☐
1 Kings 21   **PROPHETS** ☐
Psalm 119:121–144   **WRITINGS** ☐
John 4:31–54 (1 Thessalonians 5)   **APOSTLES** ☐

CANDLE LIGHTING TIMES: _____

TODAY IN HISTORY: Death of Christian Zionist pioneer Reverend William Hechler (z"l) in 5691 (1931). Hechler was an Anglican clergyman and writer who introduced Theodor Herzl to Kaiser Wilhelm II of Germany, becoming the first to give Herzl and Zionism political legitimacy. In 1897, Herzl invited him to the First Zionist Congress in Basel, Switzerland, calling him the "first Christian Zionist." The two remained friends and Hechler recorded Herzl's last words, "Greet Palestine for me. I gave my heart's blood for my people."

BESHALACH (WHEN HE SENT)

4 Feb. / 13 Shvat
SHABBAT SHIRAH
(SABBATH OF SONG)

TODAY IN HISTORY: *Shabbat Shirah* (Sabbath of Song) is the Sabbath when the Torah portion *Beshalach* is read. It contains the triumphant "Song at the Sea" from Exodus 15, as well as the "Song of Deborah" (Jdg. 5) in the accompanying *Haftarah* from the Prophets.

BESHALACH (WHEN HE SENT)

5 Feb. / 14 Shvat
SUNDAY

Exodus 18:1–12   **TORAH** ☐
1 Kings 22   **PROPHETS** ☐
Psalm 119:145–176   **WRITINGS** ☐
John 5 (2 Thessalonians 1–2)   **APOSTLES** ☐

YITRO (JETHRO)

6 Feb. / 15 Shvat

TODAY IN HISTORY: In the Torah, God instructs that the fruit from newly planted trees is forbidden for three years (Lev. 19:23–25). Instead of counting the age of each individual tree, all are counted from the 15th of Shvat (*Tu Bishvat*)—the new year of the trees. Today, *Tu Bishvat* is celebrated with a festive meal patterned after the Passover seder with a special focus on the Land of Israel, its fruit and by planting trees in Israel.

YITRO (JETHRO)

7 Feb. / 16 Shvat
TUESDAY ○

YITRO (JETHRO)

□ **TORAH** Exodus 19:1–6
□ **PROPHETS** 2 Kings 4
□ **WRITINGS** Psalm 124–125
□ **APOSTLES** John 7:1–24 (1 Timothy 2)

8 Feb. / 17 Shvat
WEDNESDAY

9 Feb. / 18 Shvat
THURSDAY

YITRO (JETHRO)

10 Feb. / 19 Shvat
FRIDAY

CANDLE LIGHTING TIMES:

YITRO (JETHRO)

11 Feb. / 20 Shvat
SHABBAT

Exodus 20:18–26[15–23] **TORAH** ☐
Isaiah 6:1–7:6, 9:6–7[5–6] **HAFTARAH** ☐
Matthew 5:13–20 **APOSTLES** ☐

_____

_____

_____

_____

_____

_____

_____

_____

_____

_____

_____

_____

_____

_____

_____

_____

_____

_____

_____

TODAY IN HISTORY: Birth of Asher (tradition, Gen. 30:12–13). "Leah's maid Zilpah bore Jacob a second son. Then Leah said, 'Happy am I! For women will call me happy.' So she named him Asher."

YITRO (JETHRO)

□ **TORAH**   Exodus 21:1–19
□ **PROPHETS** 2 Kings 7
□ **WRITINGS** Psalm 130–131
□ **APOSTLES** John 8:31–59 (1 Timothy 5)

12 Feb. / 21 Shvat
SUNDAY

13 Feb. / 22 Shvat
MONDAY ◑

MISHPATIM (JUDGMENTS)

14 Feb. / 23 Shvat
TUESDAY

TODAY IN HISTORY: The Tribes of Israel go to war with Benjamin (tradition, Judges 19–20).

MISHPATIM (JUDGMENTS)

15 Feb. / 24 Shvat
WEDNESDAY

Exodus 22:28[27]–23:5 **TORAH** ☐
2 Kings 10 **PROPHETS** ☐
Psalm 136 **WRITINGS** ☐
John 11:1–27 (2 Timothy 2) **APOSTLES** ☐

TODAY IN HISTORY: Zechariah sees a vision of a rider among the myrtle trees (Zec. 1:7). "On the twenty-fourth day of the eleventh month, which is the month Shebat, in the second year of Darius, the word of the LORD came to Zechariah the prophet…" Death of the "Even Zohar," the Messianic pioneer Yechiel Tzvi Lichtenstein (zt"l) year 5672 (1912 CE). Yechiel Lichtenstein, born 1831, came from a Chasidic background. While in Yeshiva, he became a disciple of Yeshua of Nazareth. He served at the Institutum Judaicum Delitzschianum as a professor of rabbinics and wrote several books and commentaries including an important commentary of the NT in Hebrew. His grave stone reads: "Here rests a disciple of Yeshua the Messiah, in spirit a member of the Jerusalem assembly…May his memory be a blessing" (vineofdavid.org).

MISHPATIM (JUDGMENTS)

☐ **TORAH**   Exodus 23:6–19
☐ **PROPHETS** 2 Kings 11–12
☐ **WRITINGS**   Psalm 137
☐ **APOSTLES** John 11:28–57 (2 Timothy 3)

16 Feb. / 25 Shvat
THURSDAY

17 Feb. / 26 Shvat
FRIDAY

Exodus 23:20–25   **TORAH** ☐
2 Kings 13   **PROPHETS** ☐
Psalm 138   **WRITINGS** ☐
John 12:1–19 (2 Timothy 4)   **APOSTLES** ☐

CANDLE LIGHTING TIMES:

MISHPATIM (JUDGMENTS)

☐ **TORAH** Exodus 23:26–24:18; 30:11–16

☐ **HAFTARAH** 2 Kings 12:1–16[17]

☐ **APOSTLES** Matthew 17:22–27

18 Feb. / 27 Shvat

SHABBAT SHKALIM
(SABBATH OF SHEKELS)

TODAY IN HISTORY: *Shabbat Shkalim* (Sabbath of Shekels) is the Sabbath that falls on or before the 1st of Adar (or in a leap year, before the 1st of Adar II). It adds a special reading from Exodus 30:11–16 to remind the men of Israel to contribute half a shekel for the upkeep of the Temple in time for Passover. In Temple times, as in Matthew 17:24–27, this collection of funds was gathered during this time of year.

MISHPATIM (JUDGMENTS)

19 Feb. / 28 Shvat
SUNDAY

Exodus 25:1–16 **TORAH** ☐
2 Kings 14 **PROPHETS** ☐
Psalm 139 **WRITINGS** ☐
John 12:20–50 (Titus 1) **APOSTLES** ☐

TRUMAH (HEAVE OFFERING)

☐ **TORAH**   Exodus 25:17–30
☐ **PROPHETS**   2 Kings 15–16
☐ **WRITINGS**   Psalm 140
☐ **APOSTLES**   John 13 (Titus 2)

20 Feb. / 29 Shvat
MONDAY

21 Feb. / 30 Shvat

TUESDAY ●
ROSH CHODESH (DAY 1)

Exodus 25:31–26:14 **TORAH** ☐
Numbers 28:11–15
2 Kings 17 **PROPHETS** ☐
Psalm 141–142 **WRITINGS** ☐
John 14 (Titus 3) **APOSTLES** ☐

TRUMAH (HEAVE OFFERING)

22 Feb. / 1 Adar

● WEDNESDAY
ROSH CHODESH (DAY 2)

TODAY IN HISTORY: The ninth plague—darkness—descends on Egypt (tradition, Ex. 10:21–23). "Then the LORD said to Moses, 'Stretch out your hand toward the sky, that there may be darkness over the land of Egypt, even a darkness which may be felt.'" The Prophet Ezekiel receives one of seven prophecies (nearly all dated) against Egypt. "In the twelfth year, in the twelfth month, on the first of the month, the word of the LORD came to me saying, 'Son of man, take up a lamentation over Pharaoh king of Egypt'" (Eze 32:1–2).

TRUMAH (HEAVE OFFERING)

23 Feb. / 2 Adar
THURSDAY

Exodus 26:31–37   **TORAH** ☐
2 Kings 19   **PROPHETS** ☐
Psalm 144   **WRITINGS** ☐
John 16 (Hebrews 1)   **APOSTLES** ☐

TODAY IN HISTORY: Messiah pays the half-shekel tax (possible date, Mt. 17:24–27). "When they came to Capernaum, those who collected the two-drachma tax came to Peter and said, 'Does your teacher not pay the two-drachma tax?' He said, 'Yes.'"

TRUMAH (HEAVE OFFERING)

☐ **TORAH**   Exodus 27:1–8
☐ **PROPHETS** 2 Kings 20
☐ **WRITINGS** Psalm 145
☐ **APOSTLES** John 17 (Hebrews 2)

24 Feb. / 3 Adar
FRIDAY

CANDLE LIGHTING TIMES:

TODAY IN HISTORY: The second Temple is completed (Ezr. 6:15). "This temple was completed on the third day of the month Adar; it was the sixth year of the reign of King Darius."

TRUMAH (HEAVE OFFERING)

25 Feb. / 4 Adar

SHABBAT

Exodus 27:9–19   **TORAH** ☐

1 Kings 5:12[26]–6:13   **HAFTARAH** ☐

Hebrews 8:1–6   **APOSTLES** ☐

TRUMAH (HEAVE OFFERING)

☐ **TORAH** Exodus 27:20–28:12
☐ **PROPHETS** 2 Kings 21–22
☐ **WRITINGS** Psalm 146
☐ **APOSTLES** John 18 (Hebrews 3)

26 Feb. / 5 Adar
SUNDAY

TODAY IN HISTORY: Moses last day of leadership (tradition, Dt. 34).

TETZAVEH (YOU SHALL COMMAND)

27 Feb. / 6 Adar
MONDAY ◑

Exodus 28:13–30 **TORAH** ☐
2 Kings 23 **PROPHETS** ☐
Psalm 147 **WRITINGS** ☐
John 19 (Hebrews 4) **APOSTLES** ☐

TODAY IN HISTORY: Moses completes the writing of the Torah (tradition).

TETZAVEH (YOU SHALL COMMAND)

☐ **TORAH**   Exodus 28:31–43
☐ **PROPHETS**   2 Kings 24
☐ **WRITINGS**   Psalm 148
☐ **APOSTLES**   John 20 (Hebrews 5)

28 Feb. / 7 Adar
TUESDAY

TODAY IN HISTORY: Birth of Moses (tradition, Ex. 2:1–2). "Now a man from the house of Levi went and married a daughter of Levi. The woman conceived and bore a son; and when she saw that he was beautiful, she hid him for three months." Death of Moses (tradition, Dt. 34:5–6). "So Moses the servant of the LORD died there in the land of Moab, according to the word of the LORD. And He buried him in the valley in the land of Moab, opposite Beth-peor; but no man knows his burial place to this day."

TETZAVEH (YOU SHALL COMMAND)

1 Mar. / 8 Adar
WEDNESDAY

Exodus 29:1–18   **TORAH** ☐
2 Kings 25   **PROPHETS** ☐
Psalm 149–150   **WRITINGS** ☐
John 21 (Hebrews 6)   **APOSTLES** ☐

TETZAVEH (YOU SHALL COMMAND)

□ **TORAH** Exodus 29:19–37
□ **PROPHETS** Isaiah 1
□ **WRITINGS** Proverbs 1
□ **APOSTLES** Acts 1 (Hebrews 7)

2 Mar. / 9 Adar
THURSDAY

3 Mar. / 10 Adar
FRIDAY

Exodus 29:38–46   **TORAH** ☐
Isaiah 2   **PROPHETS** ☐
Proverbs 2   **WRITINGS** ☐
Acts 2 (Hebrews 8)   **APOSTLES** ☐

CANDLE LIGHTING TIMES:

TETZAVEH (YOU SHALL COMMAND)

4 Mar. / 11 Adar
SHABBAT ZACHOR
(SABBATH OF REMEMBRANCE)

TODAY IN HISTORY: *Shabbat Zachor* (Sabbath of Remembrance) is the Sabbath right before Purim. Deuteronomy 25:17–19, describing the attack by Amalek, is recounted since Haman the Agagite most likely descended from Amalek.

TETZAVEH (YOU SHALL COMMAND)

5 Mar. / 12 Adar
SUNDAY

Exodus 30:11–31:17   **TORAH** ☐
Isaiah 3–4   **PROPHETS** ☐
Proverbs 3   **WRITINGS** ☐
Acts 3 (Hebrews 9)   **APOSTLES** ☐

TODAY IN HISTORY: The Temple is dedicated after Herod's renovations (tradition, 11 BCE).

KI TISA (WHEN YOU COUNT)

☐ **TORAH**	Exodus 31:18–33:11	
☐ **PROPHETS**	Isaiah 5	
☐ **WRITINGS**	Proverbs 4	
☐ **APOSTLES**	Acts 4 (Hebrews 10)	
☐ **SYNAGOGUE READINGS**		

6 Mar. / 13 Adar
MONDAY
TA'ANIT ESTHER (FAST OF ESTHER)
PURIM EVE

Exodus 32:11–14; 34:1–10; Isaiah 55:6–56:8 (afternoon)

TODAY IN HISTORY: The Fast of Esther (*Ta'anit Ester*) is a shorter, traditional fast on the Jewish calendar that lasts from sunrise to sunset. Normally observed on the 13th of Adar, the fast is moved to the preceding Thursday if it falls on Shabbat. The Fast of Esther is not one of the four fast days established in the Prophets (Zec. 8:19). It is a tradition commemorating the three-day fast observed by Esther and the Jewish people to be delivered from Haman's evil plot. "Go, assemble all the Jews who are found in Susa, and fast for me; do not eat or drink for three days, night or day. I and my maidens also will fast in the same way. And thus I will go in to the king, which is not according to the law; and if I perish, I perish" (Est. 4:15–16). This fast was an emergency originally observed on Passover, 14–16 Nisan (Est. 3:12f).   Haman's evil plan is put into action (Est. 3:13). "Letters were sent by couriers to all the king's provinces to destroy, to kill and to annihilate all the Jews, both young and old, women and children, in one day, the thirteenth day of the twelfth month, which is the month Adar, and to seize their possessions as plunder."   The Jews are given the right to protect themselves (Est. 8:12–13). "A copy of the edict to be issued as law in each and every province was published to all the peoples, so that the Jews would be ready for this day to avenge themselves on their enemies."

KI TISA (WHEN YOU COUNT)

7 Mar. / 14 Adar

TUESDAY ○
PURIM

Exodus 17:8–16 **TORAH** ☐
Esther 1–10 **WRITINGS** ☐
Revelation 19:1–5 **APOSTLES** ☐

TODAY IN HISTORY: The Jews feast and rejoice for the victory over their enemies (Est. 9:17). "This was done on the thirteenth day of the month Adar, and on the fourteenth day rested and made it a day of feasting and rejoicing."   The circumcision of Moses (tradition).

KI TISA (WHEN YOU COUNT)

□ **TORAH** Exodus 33:12–16; 17:8–16
□ **PROPHETS** Isaiah 6–7
□ **WRITINGS** Proverbs 5
□ **APOSTLES** Acts 5 (Hebrews 11)

8 Mar. / 15 Adar
WEDNESDAY
SHUSHAN PURIM (IN JERUSALEM)

TODAY IN HISTORY: The Jews in the capitol Shushan feast and rejoice for the victory over their enemies (Est. 9:18). "But the Jews who were in Susa assembled on the thirteenth and the fourteenth of the same month, and they rested on the fifteenth day and made it a day of feasting and rejoicing."   The Prophet Ezekiel receives one of seven prophecies (nearly all dated) against Egypt (probable date, Eze. 32:17f). "In the twelfth year, on the fifteenth of the [twelfth] month, the word of the LORD came to me saying, 'Son of man, wail for the hordes of Egypt…'"   To the joy of the Jews, King Agrippa I (brother of Bernice, cf. Ac. 25:13f) begins repairing and building the walls of Jerusalem (tradition, c. 41 CE).

KI TISA (WHEN YOU COUNT)

9 Mar. / 16 Adar
THURSDAY

Exodus 33:17–23   TORAH ☐
Isaiah 8   PROPHETS ☐
Proverbs 6   WRITINGS ☐
Acts 6 (Hebrews 12)   APOSTLES ☐

KI TISA (WHEN YOU COUNT)

☐ **TORAH** Exodus 34:1–9
☐ **PROPHETS** Isaiah 9
☐ **WRITINGS** Proverbs 7
☐ **APOSTLES** Acts 7:1–29 (Hebrews 13)

10 Mar. / 17 Adar
FRIDAY

CANDLE LIGHTING TIMES:

KI TISA (WHEN YOU COUNT)

11 Mar. / 18 Adar

SHABBAT PARAH
(RED HEIFER SABBATH)

Exodus 34:10–35   **TORAH** ☐
Numbers 19:1–22
Ezekiel 36:16–38   **HAFTARAH** ☐
Hebrews 9:11–15   **APOSTLES** ☐

_____

_____

_____

_____

_____

_____

_____

_____

_____

_____

_____

_____

_____

_____

_____

_____

_____

TODAY IN HISTORY: _Shabbat Parah_ (Red Heifer Sabbath) is the next to last Sabbath before the month of Nisan. A special reading of Numbers 19:1–22 is added in memory of the red heifer, since it is the basis for the Temple purity rituals needed in order to participate in the Passover sacrifice, as mentioned in John 11:55, "Now the Passover of the Jews was near, and many went up to Jerusalem out of the country before the Passover to purify themselves."

KI TISA (WHEN YOU COUNT)

☐ **TORAH** Exodus 35:1–29
☐ **PROPHETS** Isaiah 10
☐ **WRITINGS** Proverbs 8
☐ **APOSTLES** Acts 7:30–60 (Revelation 1)

12 Mar. / 19 Adar
SUNDAY

13 Mar. / 20 Adar
MONDAY

15 Mar. / 22 Adar
WEDNESDAY ◑

Exodus 38:1–39:1 **TORAH** ☐
Isaiah 14 **PROPHETS** ☐
Proverbs 11 **WRITINGS** ☐
Acts 10 (Revelation 4) **APOSTLES** ☐

VAYAK'HEL (HE ASSEMBLED) / PEKUDEI (COUNTINGS)

☐ **TORAH** Exodus 39:2–21
☐ **PROPHETS** Isaiah 15–16
☐ **WRITINGS** Proverbs 12
☐ **APOSTLES** Acts 11 (Revelation 5)

16 Mar. / 23 Adar
THURSDAY

17 Mar. / 24 Adar
FRIDAY

Exodus 39:22–43 **TORAH** ☐
Isaiah 17–18 **PROPHETS** ☐
Proverbs 13 **WRITINGS** ☐
Acts 12 (Revelation 6) **APOSTLES** ☐

CANDLE LIGHTING TIMES: _____

VAYAK'HEL (HE ASSEMBLED) / PEKUDEI (COUNTINGS)

18 Mar. / 25 Adar
SHABBAT HACHODESH
(SABBATH OF THE NEW MONTH)

TODAY IN HISTORY: *Shabbat HaChodesh* (Sabbath of the New Month) is the last Sabbath before the month of Nisan, during which Passover is celebrated. A special reading of Exodus 12:1–20, with instructions for Passover, is added. Traditionally, it was also during this time that God gave Israel their first Torah commandment, the sanctification of the new moon (Ex. 12:1–2), thus making Nisan the first month of the spiritual calendar.   King Jehoiachin is brought out of prison, apparently to be fully released two days later (Jer. 52:31–34, cf. 2 Ki. 25:27–30). "…in the twelfth month, on the twenty-fifth of the month, that Evil-merodach king of Babylon, in the first year of his reign, showed favor to Jehoiachin king of Judah and brought him out of prison."

VAYAK'HEL (HE ASSEMBLED) / PEKUDEI (COUNTINGS)

19 Mar. / 26 Adar
SUNDAY

Leviticus 1:1–13   **TORAH** ☐
Isaiah 19–20   **PROPHETS** ☐
Proverbs 14   **WRITINGS** ☐
Acts 13 (Revelation 7)   **APOSTLES** ☐

VAYIKRA (AND HE CALLED)

20 Mar. / 27 Adar
MONDAY

TODAY IN HISTORY: King Jehoiachin is released from prison (2 Ki. 25:27–30). Death of King Zedekiah (tradition, Jer. 52:11). "Then he blinded the eyes of Zedekiah; and the king of Babylon bound him with bronze fetters and brought him to Babylon and put him in prison until the day of his death."

VAYIKRA (AND HE CALLED)

21 Mar. / 28 Adar
TUESDAY

Leviticus 2:7–16   **TORAH** ☐
Isaiah 23   **PROPHETS** ☐
Proverbs 16   **WRITINGS** ☐
Acts 15 (Revelation 9)   **APOSTLES** ☐

VAYIKRA (AND HE CALLED)

☐ **TORAH**	Leviticus 3
☐ **PROPHETS**	Isaiah 24
☐ **WRITINGS**	Proverbs 17
☐ **APOSTLES**	Acts 16 (Revelation 10)

22 Mar. / 29 Adar
WEDNESDAY

VAYIKRA (AND HE CALLED)

23 Mar. / 1 Nisan

THURSDAY ●
ROSH CHODESH

Leviticus 4:1–26	**TORAH** ☐
Numbers 28:11–15	
Isaiah 25–26	**PROPHETS** ☐
Proverbs 18	**WRITINGS** ☐
Acts 17 (Revelation 11)	**APOSTLES** ☐

TODAY IN HISTORY: Israel is given their first Torah commandment (tradition, Ex. 12:1–2). "Now the LORD said to Moses and Aaron in the land of Egypt, 'This month shall be the beginning of months for you; it is to be the first month of the year to you.'" The Tabernacle is erected (Ex. 40:2,17). "Now in the first month of the second year, on the first day of the month, the tabernacle was erected." The reconsecration of the first Temple begins during King Hezekiah's reign (2 Chr. 29:17). "Now they began the consecration on the first day of the first month". The Prophet Ezekiel receives one of seven prophecies against Egypt. It is the latest dated prophecy recorded in Ezekiel. "Now in the twenty-seventh year, in the first month, on the first of the month, the word of the LORD came to me saying, 'Son of man, Nebuchadnezzar king of Babylon made his army labor hard against Tyre…'" (Eze. 29:17–18). Death of *HaYedid*, "The Friend," Christian Zionist pioneer Maj. Gen. Orde Charles Wingate (z"l) year 5704 (1944 CE). Wingate was a British intelligence officer posted to Mandatory Palestine during the Arab Revolt in the 1930s. Raised a Plymouth Brethren, he always kept a Bible on him. To the chagrin of the often antisemitic British authorities, he trained the Jewish community in professional military tactics. This "Father of the IDF" became a mentor to Moshe Dayan and a personal friend of Weizmann and Ben Gurion. After his death fighting the Japanese in Burma, the Yeshurun Synagogue in Jerusalem composed a special version of the *Kol Male Rachamim* prayer in his memory. "May the name of Orde Wingate be remembered in the book of redemption of the House of Israel for eternity" (fozmuseum.com).

VAYIKRA (AND HE CALLED)

☐ **TORAH**	Leviticus 4:27–5:10
☐ **PROPHETS**	Isaiah 27
☐ **WRITINGS**	Proverbs 19
☐ **APOSTLES**	Acts 18 (Revelation 12)

24 Mar. / 2 Nisan

FRIDAY

CANDLE LIGHTING TIMES:

TODAY IN HISTORY: The first red heifer is prepared (tradition, Num. 19:1–22). "Speak to the sons of Israel that they bring you an unblemished red heifer in which is no defect and on which a yoke has never been placed."

VAYIKRA (AND HE CALLED)

25 Mar. / 3 Nisan
SHABBAT

Leviticus 5:11–6:7[5:26] **TORAH** ☐
Isaiah 43:21–44:23 **HAFTARAH** ☐
Hebrews 13:10–16 **APOSTLES** ☐

_____

_____

_____

_____

_____

_____

_____

_____

_____

_____

_____

_____

_____

_____

_____

_____

_____

_____

_____

TODAY IN HISTORY: The Levites are ordained for service in the Tabernacle (tradition, Num. 8:5–22). "Then after that the Levites went in to perform their service in the tent of meeting before Aaron and before his sons".

VAYIKRA (AND HE CALLED)

☐ **TORAH** Leviticus 6:8–18[1–11]
☐ **PROPHETS** Isaiah 28
☐ **WRITINGS** Proverbs 20
☐ **APOSTLES** Acts 19 (Revelation 13)

26 Mar. / 4 Nisan
SUNDAY

27 Mar. / 5 Nisan
MONDAY

Leviticus 6:19[12]–7:10   **TORAH** ☐
Isaiah 29   **PROPHETS** ☐
Proverbs 21   **WRITINGS** ☐
Acts 20 (Revelation 14)   **APOSTLES** ☐

TODAY IN HISTORY: Two spies are sent to Jericho (tradition, Jos. 2:1). "Then Joshua the son of Nun sent two men as spies secretly from Shittim, saying, 'Go, view the land, especially Jericho.'"

TSAV (COMMAND)

☐ **TORAH** Leviticus 7:11–38
☐ **PROPHETS** Isaiah 30
☐ **WRITINGS** Proverbs 22
☐ **APOSTLES** Acts 21 (Revelation 15)

28 Mar. / 6 Nisan
TUESDAY

TODAY IN HISTORY: The brother of Messiah, the Apostle Yaakov HaTzadik (James the Rightous) is martyred in Jerusalem close to Passover (tradition, Josephus, *Antiquities* 20.197–201, Eusebius, *Ecclesiastical Histories* 2.23.4,10–18). "So they went up and threw down the just man [from the pinnacle of the Temple], and said to each other, 'Let us stone James the Just.' And they began to stone him, for he was not killed by the fall…But those in the city who seemed most moderate and skilled in the law were very angry at this, and sent secretly to the king, requesting him to order [the high priest] Ananus to cease such proceedings."

TSAV (COMMAND)

29 Mar. / 7 Nisan
WEDNESDAY ☽

Leviticus 8:1–13   **TORAH** ☐

Isaiah 31–32   **PROPHETS** ☐

Proverbs 23   **WRITINGS** ☐

Acts 22 (Revelation 16)   **APOSTLES** ☐

TODAY IN HISTORY: The Prophet Ezekiel receives one of seven prophecies (nearly all dated) against Egypt. "In the eleventh year, in the first month, on the seventh of the month, the word of the LORD came to me saying, 'Son of man, I have broken the arm of Pharaoh king of Egypt'" (Eze. 30:20–21).

TSAV (COMMAND)

☐ **TORAH** Leviticus 8:14–21
☐ **PROPHETS** Isaiah 33
☐ **WRITINGS** Proverbs 24
☐ **APOSTLES** Acts 23 (Revelation 17)

30 Mar. / 8 Nisan
THURSDAY

TODAY IN HISTORY: The priests enter the first Temple to reconsecrate it during King Hezekiah's reign (2 Chr. 29:17). "Now they began the consecration on the first day of the first month, and on the eighth day of the month they entered the porch of the LORD. Then they consecrated the house of the LORD in eight days, and finished on the sixteenth day of the first month."

TSAV (COMMAND)

31 Mar. / 9 Nisan
FRIDAY

CANDLE LIGHTING TIMES:

TSAV (COMMAND)

☐ **TORAH**   Leviticus 8:30–36
☐ **HAFTARAH**   Malachi 3:1–4:6[3:24]
☐ **APOSTLES**   Luke 1:13–17; 76–80

1 Apr. / 10 Nisan
SHABBAT HAGADOL
(THE GREAT SABBATH)

TODAY IN HISTORY: Messiah rides into Jerusalem, visits the Temple and returns to Bethany (Matt. 21:1–9). "The crowds going ahead of Him, and those who followed, were shouting, 'Hosanna to the Son of David; BLESSED IS HE WHO COMES IN THE NAME OF THE LORD; Hosanna in the highest!'" The Passover lambs are selected (Ex. 12:3). "Speak to all the congregation of Israel, saying, 'On the tenth of this month they are each one to take a lamb for themselves, according to their fathers' households, a lamb for each household.'" The people of Israel cross the Jordan with Joshua (Jos. 4:19). "Now the people came up from the Jordan on the tenth of the first month and camped at Gilgal on the eastern edge of Jericho." The Prophet Ezekiel sees a vision of the new Temple (possible date, Eze. 40–48). "In the twenty-fifth year of our exile, at the beginning of the year, on the tenth of the month...In the visions of God He brought me into the land of Israel and set me on a very high mountain." *Shabbat HaGadol* (The Great Sabbath) is the last Sabbath before Passover. A special reading from the Prophet Malachi is read, including the promise of Elijah's coming and the "great" day of the LORD. In the afternoon, an extensive sermon is traditionally delivered to the general community to prepare the people for Passover.

2 Apr. / 11 Nisan
SUNDAY

Exodus 33:12–16 **TORAH** ☐
Isaiah 36 **PROPHETS** ☐
Proverbs 26 **WRITINGS** ☐
Acts 25 (Revelation 19) **APOSTLES** ☐

TODAY IN HISTORY: Messiah goes to Jerusalem, curses the fig tree, and cleanses the Temple (Mt. 21:10–16). "And He entered the temple and began to drive out those who were buying and selling in the temple, and overturned the tables of the money changers and the seats of those who were selling doves; and He would not permit anyone to carry [anything] through the temple." (Mk. 11:15–16).

PESACH (PASSOVER)

☐ **TORAH** Exodus 33:17–19
☐ **PROPHETS** Isaiah 37
☐ **WRITINGS** Proverbs 27
☐ **APOSTLES** Acts 26 (Revelation 20)

3 Apr. / 12 Nisan
MONDAY

TODAY IN HISTORY: Messiah leaves Jerusalem at evening, returns in the morning, and teaches in the Temple and on the Mt. of Olives (Mt. 21:17–26:2). "When He entered the temple, the chief priests and the elders of the people came to Him while He was teaching…As He was sitting on the Mount of Olives, the disciples came to Him privately, saying, "Tell us, when will these things happen, and what will be the sign of Your coming…?"" Ezra the Scribe begins his journey to Jerusalem (Ezr. 8:31). "Then we journeyed from the river Ahava on the twelfth of the first month to go to Jerusalem."

PESACH (PASSOVER)

4 Apr. / 13 Nisan
TUESDAY

Exodus 33:20–23 **TORAH** ☐
Isaiah 38–39 **PROPHETS** ☐
Proverbs 28 **WRITINGS** ☐
Acts 27 (Revelation 21) **APOSTLES** ☐

TODAY IN HISTORY: Messiah celebrates an early Passover seder with his disciples and is later arrested (Mt. 26:17–56). "And He said to them, 'I have earnestly desired to eat this Passover with you before I suffer'" (Lk. 22:15). At evening all leaven is removed from Jewish homes (tradition, Ex. 12:15, cf. 1 Cor. 5:6–8). "Seven days you shall eat unleavened bread, but on the first day you shall remove leaven from your houses; for whoever eats anything leavened from the first day until the seventh day, that person shall be cut off from Israel." Haman drafts a decree to annihilate all the Jews on 13th of Adar, eleven months later (Est. 3). "Then the king's scribes were summoned on the thirteenth day of the first month, and it was written just as Haman commanded to the king's satraps."

PESACH (PASSOVER)

☐ **TORAH**   Exodus 34:1–3
☐ **PROPHETS**   Isaiah 53 (Messianic)
☐ **WRITINGS**   Psalm 22 (Messianic)
☐ **APOSTLES**   Mark 15; 1 Cor. 5:6–8 (Messianic)
☐ **SYNAGOGUE READINGS**
Exodus 32:11–14; 34:1–10; Isaiah 55:6–56:8

5 Apr. / 14 Nisan
WEDNESDAY
TA'ANIT BECHOROT
(FAST OF THE FIRSTBORN)
PESACH EVE

_____

_____

_____

_____

_____

_____

_____

_____

_____

_____

_____

CANDLE LIGHTING TIMES: _____

TODAY IN HISTORY: Messiah is condemned to death, executed on the cross, and buried (Mt. 26:57–27:61). "About the ninth hour Yeshua cried out in a loud voice, 'Eloi, Eloi, lama sabachthani?'—which means, 'My God, my God, why have you forsaken me?'…And when Yeshua had cried out again in a loud voice, he gave up his spirit" (NIV).   The Passover lambs are slaughtered in the afternoon (Ex. 12:6, Dt. 16:6). "You shall keep it until the fourteenth day of the same month, then the whole assembly of the congregation of Israel is to kill it [toward evening]." _Ta'anit Bechorot_ (Fast of the Firstborn) is a unique fast day on the Jewish calendar, beginning at dawn. Only firstborn Jewish men fast, done in memory and gratitude for the deliverance from the Plague of the Firstborn in Egypt. "Now it came about at midnight that the LORD struck all the firstborn in the land of Egypt, from the firstborn of Pharaoh who sat on his throne to the firstborn of the captive who was in the dungeon" (Ex. 12:29).

_____

PESACH (PASSOVER)

6 Apr. / 15 Nisan
THURSDAY ○
PESACH DAY 1 (PASSOVER)

Exodus 12:21–51   **TORAH** ☐
Numbers 28:16–25
Joshua 5:2–6:1   **HAFTARAH** ☐
1 Peter 2:19–25   **APOSTLES** ☐

_____

_____

_____

_____

_____

_____

_____

_____

_____

_____

_____

_____

_____

_____

_____

_____

CANDLE LIGHTING TIMES: _____

TODAY IN HISTORY: Barley sheaves are harvested in the evening (Lev. 23:10). "When you enter the land which I am going to give to you and reap its harvest, then you shall bring in the sheaf of the first fruits of your harvest to the priest." The people of Israel leave Egypt (Ex. 12:28–51). "And on that same day the LORD brought the sons of Israel out of the land of Egypt by their hosts."

PESACH (PASSOVER) _____

7 Apr. / 16 Nisan

FRIDAY
PESACH DAY 2* (PASSOVER)
DAY 1 OF THE OMER (FIRST FRUITS)

CANDLE LIGHTING TIMES:

TODAY IN HISTORY: Messiah rises from the dead during the night and afterwards appears to the disciples (Lk. 24). "But on the first day of the week, at early dawn, they came to the tomb…" The Omer of barley first fruits is waved in the Temple (Lev. 23:10–11). "He shall wave the sheaf before the LORD for you to be accepted; on the day after the sabbath the priest shall wave it." The reconsecration of the first Temple under King Hezekiah is finished (2 Chr. 29:17). "Then they consecrated the house of the LORD in eight days, and finished on the sixteenth day of the first month." * It is customary among the Jewish people, since ancient times, to double the festival sabbath (*yom tov*) outside Israel.

8 Apr. / 17 Nisan

SHABBAT
PESACH DAY 3 (PASSOVER)
DAY 2 OF THE OMER

Exodus 34:1–26   **TORAH** ☐
Numbers 28:19–25
Ezekiel 37:1–14   **HAFTARAH** ☐
Song of Songs 1–8   **WRITINGS** ☐
Ephesians 5:25–33   **APOSTLES** ☐

9 Apr. / 18 Nisan

SUNDAY
PESACH DAY 4 (PASSOVER)
DAY 3 OF THE OMER

10 Apr. / 19 Nisan
MONDAY
PESACH DAY 5 (PASSOVER)
DAY 4 OF THE OMER

Exodus 34:1–26 **TORAH** ☐
Numbers 28:19–25
Isaiah 41 **PROPHETS** ☐
Proverbs 30 **WRITINGS** ☐
James 1 (Matthew 1) **APOSTLES** ☐

PESACH (PASSOVER)

☐ **TORAH**	Leviticus 9:1–16
	Numbers 28:1–25
☐ **PROPHETS**	Isaiah 42
☐ **WRITINGS**	Proverbs 31
☐ **APOSTLES**	James 2 (Matthew 2)

11 Apr. / 20 Nisan
TUESDAY
PESACH DAY 6 (PASSOVER)
DAY 5 OF THE OMER

CANDLE LIGHTING TIMES:

PESACH (PASSOVER)

12 Apr. / 21 Nisan

WEDNESDAY
PESACH DAY 7 (PASSOVER)
DAY 6 OF THE OMER

Exodus 13:17–15:26 **TORAH** ☐
Numbers 28:19–25
2 Samuel 22:1–51 **HAFTARAH** ☐
Romans 6:1–11 **APOSTLES** ☐

CANDLE LIGHTING TIMES:

TODAY IN HISTORY: The people of Israel cross the Sea of Reeds (Red Sea) (tradition, Ex. 14–15). "The sons of Israel went through the midst of the sea on the dry land, and the waters were like a wall to them on their right hand and on their left."

PESACH (PASSOVER)

□ **TORAH**   Deuteronomy 15:19–16:17
                  Numbers 28:19–25
□ **HAFTARAH** Isaiah 10:32–12:6
□ **APOSTLES** Revelation 19:11–20:6

13 Apr. / 22 Nisan
◑ THURSDAY
PESACH DAY 8* (PASSOVER)
DAY 7 OF THE OMER

* It is customary among the Jewish people, since ancient times, to double the festival sabbath (*yom tov*) outside Israel.

14 Apr. / 23 Nisan

FRIDAY

DAY 8 OF THE OMER

Leviticus 9:17–23   **TORAH** ☐
Isaiah 43   **PROPHETS** ☐
Job 1   **WRITINGS** ☐
James 3 (Matthew 3)   **APOSTLES** ☐

CANDLE LIGHTING TIMES:

SHMINI (EIGHTH)

☐ **TORAH** Leviticus 9:24–11:47
☐ **HAFTARAH** 2 Samuel 6:1–7:17
☐ **APOSTLES** Hebrews 7:11–28

15 Apr. / 24 Nisan
SHABBAT
DAY 9 OF THE OMER

TODAY IN HISTORY: Messiah appears to the disciples and to Thomas (possible date, John 20:24–29). "After eight days His disciples were again inside, and Thomas with them. Yeshua came, the doors having been shut, and stood in their midst and said, 'Peace be with you.'" Daniel the Prophet sees a vision by the river Tigris (Dan. 10:4f). "On the twenty-fourth day of the first month, while I was by the bank of the great river, that is, the Tigris…"

SHMINI (EIGHTH)

16 Apr. / 25 Nisan
SUNDAY
DAY 10 OF THE OMER

Leviticus 12:1–13:23   **TORAH** ☐
Isaiah 44   **PROPHETS** ☐
Job 2   **WRITINGS** ☐
James 4 (Matthew 4)   **APOSTLES** ☐

□ **TORAH** Leviticus 13:24–39
□ **PROPHETS** Isaiah 45
□ **WRITINGS** Job 3
□ **APOSTLES** James 5 (Matthew 5)

17 Apr. / 26 Nisan
MONDAY
DAY 11 OF THE OMER

18 Apr. / 27 Nisan

TUESDAY

YOM HASHOAH
(HOLOCAUST MEMORIAL DAY)

DAY 12 OF THE OMER

Leviticus 13:40–54 **TORAH** ☐
Isaiah 46 **PROPHETS** ☐
Job 4 **WRITINGS** ☐
1 Peter 1 (Matthew 6) **APOSTLES** ☐

TODAY IN HISTORY: *Yom HaShoah* (Holocaust Memorial Day) was inaugurated by the State of Israel in 1953. It falls eight days before Israel Independence Day and was originally planned as a commemoration connected with the Warsaw Ghetto Uprising that started the 14th of Nisan (April 19, 1943). At 10:00 a.m. sirens sound throughout Israel and most of the country and traffic come to a complete stop observing 2 minutes of standing silence. Many religious commemorate the Holocaust on the Fast of Tevet and the Ninth of Av.   Death of Joshua (tradition, Jos. 24:29). "It came about after these things that Joshua the son of Nun, the servant of the LORD, died, being one hundred and ten years old."

TAZRIA (SHE WILL CONCEIVE) METZORA (LEPER)

☐ **TORAH**	Leviticus 13:55–14:20
☐ **PROPHETS**	Isaiah 47
☐ **WRITINGS**	Job 5
☐ **APOSTLES**	1 Peter 2 (Matthew 7)

19 Apr. / 28 Nisan
WEDNESDAY
DAY 13 OF THE OMER

TODAY IN HISTORY: The walls of Jericho fall (tradition, Jos. 6:20). "…the people shouted with a great shout and the wall fell down flat, so that the people went up into the city, every man straight ahead, and they took the city."

TAZRIA (SHE WILL CONCEIVE) METZORA (LEPER)

20 Apr. / 29 Nisan

THURSDAY
DAY 14 OF THE OMER

Leviticus 14:21–32   **TORAH** ☐
Isaiah 48   **PROPHETS** ☐
Job 6   **WRITINGS** ☐
1 Peter 3 (Matthew 8)   **APOSTLES** ☐

TAZRIA (SHE WILL CONCEIVE) METZORA (LEPER)

21 Apr. / 30 Nisan

● FRIDAY
ROSH CHODESH (DAY 1)
DAY 15 OF THE OMER

CANDLE LIGHTING TIMES:

TAZRIA (SHE WILL CONCEIVE) METZORA (LEPER)

22 Apr. / 1 Iyar

SHABBAT ●
ROSH CHODESH (DAY 2)
DAY 16 OF THE OMER

Leviticus 15:16–33   **TORAH** ☐
Numbers 28:9–15
Isaiah 66:1–24   **HAFTARAH** ☐
Revelation 21:1–8   **APOSTLES** ☐

TODAY IN HISTORY: Moses takes a census of the people in the wilderness (Num. 1:1f). "Then the LORD spoke to Moses in the wilderness of Sinai, in the tent of meeting, on the first of the second month, in the second year after they had come out of the land of Egypt, saying, 'Take a census…'" Construction on the second Temple begins (Ezr. 3:8). "Now in the second year of their coming to the house of God at Jerusalem in the second month, Zerubbabel the son of Shealtiel and Jeshua the son of Jozadak and the rest of their brothers…began the work…"

TAZRIA (SHE WILL CONCEIVE) METZORA (LEPER)

☐ **TORAH**	Leviticus 16:1–24
☐ **PROPHETS**	Isaiah 50
☐ **WRITINGS**	Job 8
☐ **APOSTLES**	1 Peter 5 (Matthew 10)

23 Apr. / 2 Iyar
SUNDAY
DAY 17 OF THE OMER

TODAY IN HISTORY: Construction begins on the first Temple (2 Chr. 3:1f). "Then Solomon began to build the house of the LORD in Jerusalem on Mount Moriah…He began to build on the second day in the second month of the fourth year of his reign." Messiah appears to the disciples in conjunction with the miracle catch of the 153 fish (possible date, Jn. 21). "Afterward Yeshua appeared again to his disciples, by the Sea of Tiberias. It happened this way…" (NIV).

ACHAREI MOT (AFTER THE DEATH) / KEDOSHIM (HOLY)

24 Apr. / 3 Iyar

MONDAY
DAY 18 OF THE OMER

Leviticus 16:25–17:7 **TORAH** ☐
Isaiah 51 **PROPHETS** ☐
Job 9 **WRITINGS** ☐
2 Peter 1 (Matthew 11) **APOSTLES** ☐

ACHAREI MOT (AFTER THE DEATH) / KEDOSHIM (HOLY)

25 Apr. / 4 Iyar

TUESDAY
YOM HAZIKARON
(MEMORIAL DAY)
DAY 19 OF THE OMER

TODAY IN HISTORY: *Yom HaZikaron* (Memorial Day), whose full title is "Day of Remembrance for the Fallen Soldiers of Israel and Victims of Terrorism" was established by Israel in 1963 and is Israel's official Memorial Day. At 8:00 p.m. on the Eve of *Yom HaZikaron*, sirens sound throughout Israel and most of the country and traffic come to a complete stop observing 1 minute of standing silence. At 11:00 a.m., the siren sounds for 2 minutes and again the nation stops to remember at memorial ceremonies across the country. Normally observed on the 4th of Iyar, it may be moved earlier or postponed if its observance would conflict with Shabbat.

ACHAREI MOT (AFTER THE DEATH) / KEDOSHIM (HOLY)

26 Apr. / 5 Iyar
WEDNESDAY
YOM HA'ATZMAUT
(ISRAEL INDEPENDENCE DAY)
DAY 20 OF THE OMER

Leviticus 18:22–19:14 **TORAH** ☐
Isaiah 54 **PROPHETS** ☐
Job 11 **WRITINGS** ☐
2 Peter 3 (Matthew 12: 22–50) **APOSTLES** ☐

TODAY IN HISTORY: The British Mandate over Palestine expires, and the Jewish People's Council, lead by David Ben-Gurion, gather at the Tel Aviv Museum and declare the establishment of the State of Israel. "By virtue of our natural and historic right and on the strength of the resolution of the United Nations General Assembly, [we] hereby declare the establishment of a Jewish state in Eretz-Israel, to be known as the State of Israel…The State of Israel will be open for Jewish immigration and for the Ingathering of the Exiles…it will be based on freedom, justice and peace as envisaged by the prophets of Israel…Placing our trust in the 'Rock of Israel,' we affix our signatures to this proclamation…on this Sabbath eve, the 5th of Iyar, 5708 (May 14, 1948)." The new state is recognized that night by the United States, soon followed by the USSR, and is simultaneously attacked by five Arab states.   *Yom Ha'Atzmaut* (Israel Independence Day) is normally observed on the 5th of Iyar, but may be moved earlier or postponed if its observance would conflict with Shabbat.

ACHAREI MOT (AFTER THE DEATH) / KEDOSHIM (HOLY)

☐ **TORAH** Leviticus 19:15–32
☐ **PROPHETS** Isaiah 55–56
☐ **WRITINGS** Job 12
☐ **APOSTLES** 1 John 1–2:11 (Matthew 13:1–30)

27 Apr. / 6 Iyar
◐ THURSDAY
DAY 21 OF THE OMER

28 Apr. / 7 Iyar

FRIDAY

DAY 22 OF THE OMER

Leviticus 19:33–20:7 **TORAH** ☐

Isaiah 57 **PROPHETS** ☐

Job 13 **WRITINGS** ☐

1 John 2:12–29 (Matthew 13:31–58) **APOSTLES** ☐

CANDLE LIGHTING TIMES:

ACHAREI MOT (AFTER THE DEATH) / KEDOSHIM (HOLY)

☐ **TORAH** Leviticus 20:8–27
☐ **HAFTARAH** Amos 9:7–15
☐ **APOSTLES** Acts 15:13–33

29 Apr. / 8 Iyar
SHABBAT
DAY 23 OF THE OMER

ACHAREI MOT (AFTER THE DEATH) / KEDOSHIM (HOLY)

30 Apr. / 9 Iyar

SUNDAY
DAY 24 OF THE OMER

Leviticus 21:1–15 **TORAH** ☐
Isaiah 58 **PROPHETS** ☐
Job 14 **WRITINGS** ☐
1 John 3 (Matthew 14) **APOSTLES** ☐

EMOR (SPEAK)

□ **TORAH**   Leviticus 21:16–22:16
□ **PROPHETS**   Isaiah 59
□ **WRITINGS**   Job 15
□ **APOSTLES**   1 John 4 (Matthew 15)

1 May / 10 Iyar
MONDAY
DAY 25 OF THE OMER

TODAY IN HISTORY: Death of Eli the High Priest (tradition, 1 Sam. 4:18). "When he mentioned the ark of God, Eli fell off the seat backward beside the gate, and his neck was broken and he died, for he was old and heavy. Thus he judged Israel forty years."

EMOR (SPEAK)

2 May / 11 Iyar

TUESDAY

DAY 26 OF THE OMER

Leviticus 22:17–33 **TORAH** ☐

Isaiah 60 **PROPHETS** ☐

Job 16 **WRITINGS** ☐

1 John 5 (Matthew 16) **APOSTLES** ☐

EMOR (SPEAK)

☐ **TORAH**	Leviticus 23:1–22	
☐ **PROPHETS**	Isaiah 61–62	
☐ **WRITINGS**	Job 17	
☐ **APOSTLES**	2 John (Matthew 17)	

3 May / 12 Iyar
WEDNESDAY
DAY 27 OF THE OMER

4 May / 13 Iyar
THURSDAY
DAY 28 OF THE OMER

Leviticus 23:23–32 **TORAH** ☐
Isaiah 63–64 **PROPHETS** ☐
Job 18 **WRITINGS** ☐
3 John (Matthew 18) **APOSTLES** ☐

EMOR (SPEAK)

☐ **TORAH**   Leviticus 23:33–44
☐ **PROPHETS** Isaiah 65
☐ **WRITINGS** Job 19
☐ **APOSTLES** Jude (Matthew 19)

5 May / 14 Iyar
○ FRIDAY
PESACH SHENI
(SECOND PASSOVER)
DAY 29 OF THE OMER

CANDLE LIGHTING TIMES:

TODAY IN HISTORY: Joseph of Arimathea and Nicodemus celebrate *Pesach Sheni* (Jn. 19:38–42). "After these things Joseph of Arimathea, being a disciple of Yeshua, but a secret one for fear of the Jews, asked Pilate that he might take away the body of Yeshua; and Pilate granted permission. So he came and took away His body. Nicodemus, who had first come to Him by night, also came…" *Pesach Sheni* (Second Passover, Num. 9:6–14). "If any one of you or of your generations becomes unclean because of a dead person, or is on a distant journey, he may, however, observe the Passover to the LORD. In the second month on the fourteenth day at twilight, they shall observe it". King Hezekiah and all Israel celebrate *Pesach Sheni* for 14 days (2 Chr. 30:1f). "For the king and his princes and all the assembly in Jerusalem had decided to celebrate the Passover in the second month, since they could not celebrate it at that time".

EMOR (SPEAK)

6 May / 15 Iyar

SHABBAT
DAY 30 OF THE OMER

Leviticus 24 **TORAH** ☐
Ezekiel 44:15–31 **HAFTARAH** ☐
Luke 12:35–48 **APOSTLES** ☐

TODAY IN HISTORY: The people of Israel arrive in the wilderness of Sin (Ex. 16:1). "Then they set out from Elim, and all the congregation of the sons of Israel came to the wilderness of Sin, which is between Elim and Sinai, on the fifteenth day of the second month after their departure from the land of Egypt."

EMOR (SPEAK)

☐ **TORAH**   Leviticus 25:1–18
☐ **PROPHETS** Isaiah 66
☐ **WRITINGS** Job 20
☐ **APOSTLES** Romans 1 (Matthew 20)

7 May / 16 Iyar
SUNDAY
DAY 31 OF THE OMER

8 May / 17 Iyar

MONDAY
DAY 32 OF THE OMER

Leviticus 25:19–28   **TORAH** ☐
Jeremiah 1   **PROPHETS** ☐
Job 21   **WRITINGS** ☐
Romans 2 (Matthew 21)   **APOSTLES** ☐

BEHAR (ON THE MOUNTAIN) / BECHUKOTAI (IN MY STATUTES)

9 May / 18 Iyar
TUESDAY
DAY 33 OF THE OMER (*LAG BA'OMER*)

TODAY IN HISTORY: The manna begins to fall from heaven (tradition, Ex. 16:1–4). "Behold, I will rain bread from heaven for you; and the people shall go out and gather a day's portion every day, that I may test them, whether or not they will walk in My Torah." *Lag Ba'Omer* is a minor Jewish holiday celebrated on the 33rd day (*Lag* in Hebrew) of the Omer-counting. Celebrations famously include lighting bonfires in the evening. Tradition says that during the second Jewish revolt against the Romans (132-135 CE), a plague, which killed 24,000 disciples of the famous Rabbi Akiva, ceased on this day (*b.Yevamot* 62b). The end of the plague is likely a veiled reference to a successful turn in the military revolt. It is also the traditional memorial of the death of Akiva's greatest disciple, Rabbi Shimon bar Yochai. Consequently, the bonfires symbolize both the Jewish fighting spirit and the light of Torah teaching.

BEHAR (ON THE MOUNTAIN) / BECHUKOTAI (IN MY STATUTES)

10 May / 19 Iyar

WEDNESDAY

DAY 34 OF THE OMER

Leviticus 25:39–26:9   **TORAH** ☐
Jeremiah 3   **PROPHETS** ☐
Job 23   **WRITINGS** ☐
Romans 4 (Matthew 23)   **APOSTLES** ☐

BEHAR (ON THE MOUNTAIN) / BECHUKOTAI (IN MY STATUTES)

☐ **TORAH**   Leviticus 26:10–46
☐ **PROPHETS**   Jeremiah 4
☐ **WRITINGS**   Job 24
☐ **APOSTLES**   Romans 5 (Matthew 24:1-28)

11 May / 20 Iyar
THURSDAY
DAY 35 OF THE OMER

TODAY IN HISTORY: The people of Israel leave Sinai the year following the Exodus (Num. 10:11–13). "Now in the second year, in the second month, on the twentieth of the month, the cloud was lifted from over the tabernacle of the testimony; and the sons of Israel set out on their journeys from the wilderness of Sinai."

BEHAR (ON THE MOUNTAIN) / BECHUKOTAI (IN MY STATUTES)

12 May / 21 Iyar

FRIDAY ◐
DAY 36 OF THE OMER

Leviticus 27:1–15 **TORAH** ☐
Jeremiah 5 **PROPHETS** ☐
Job 25–26 **WRITINGS** ☐
Romans 6 (Matthew 24:29–51) **APOSTLES** ☐

CANDLE LIGHTING TIMES:

BEHAR (ON THE MOUNTAIN) / BECHUKOTAI (IN MY STATUTES)

☐ **TORAH**   Leviticus 27:16–34
☐ **HAFTARAH**   Jeremiah 16:19–17:14
☐ **APOSTLES**   John 14:15–27

13 May / 22 Iyar
SHABBAT
DAY 37 OF THE OMER

TODAY IN HISTORY: The commandment of Sabbath is given (tradition, Ex. 16:23–29). "This is what the LORD commanded: 'Tomorrow is to be a day of rest, a holy Sabbath to the LORD. So bake what you want to bake and boil what you want to boil. Save whatever is left and keep it until morning'" (NIV).

BEHAR (ON THE MOUNTAIN) / BECHUKOTAI (IN MY STATUTES)

14 May / 23 Iyar
SUNDAY
DAY 38 OF THE OMER

Numbers 1:1–19 **TORAH** ☐
Jeremiah 6 **PROPHETS** ☐
Job 27 **WRITINGS** ☐
Romans 7 (Matthew 25) **APOSTLES** ☐

TODAY IN HISTORY: Water comes from the rock at Horeb (tradition, Ex. 17:1–7). "'Behold, I will stand before you there on the rock at Horeb; and you shall strike the rock, and water will come out of it, that the people may drink.' And Moses did so in the sight of the elders of Israel." Death of Christian Zionist and Messianic pioneer Count Von Zinzendorf (zt"l) 5520 (1760). Zinzendorf was a German missions pioneer and a leading 18th century Protestant. He had a vision for the national and spiritual restoration of Israel in her land. As a "firstfruits" of this vision, he encouraged the establishment of *Judenkehille* (Jews' *kehilla*)—Torah-observant Messianic Jewish communities existing autonomously within the Jewish community, rather than in Gentile churches. By the 1770s, *Judenkehille* existed in Germany, England, and Switzerland.

BAMIDBAR (IN THE WILDERNESS)

☐ **TORAH** Numbers 1:20–54
☐ **PROPHETS** Jeremiah 7
☐ **WRITINGS** Job 28
☐ **APOSTLES** Romans 8 (Matthew 26:1–35)

15 May / 24 Iyar
MONDAY
DAY 39 OF THE OMER

16 May / 25 Iyar

TUESDAY
ASCENSION OF MESSIAH

DAY 40 OF THE OMER

Numbers 2   **TORAH** ☐
Jeremiah 8   **PROPHETS** ☐
Job 29   **WRITINGS** ☐
Romans 9 (Matthew 26:36–75)   **APOSTLES** ☐
Acts 1:1–12 (Messianic Reading)

TODAY IN HISTORY: Messiah ascends from the Mt. of Olives (Ac. 1:1–12). "He appeared to them over a period of forty days and spoke about the kingdom of God… He was taken up before their very eyes, and a cloud hid him from their sight… 'This same Yeshua, who has been taken from you into heaven, will come back in the same way you have seen him go into heaven'" (NIV).

BAMIDBAR (IN THE WILDERNESS)

☐ **TORAH**   Numbers 3:1–13
☐ **PROPHETS**   Jeremiah 9
☐ **WRITINGS**   Job 30
☐ **APOSTLES**   Romans 10 (Matthew 27:1–31)

17 May / 26 Iyar
WEDNESDAY
DAY 41 OF THE OMER

TODAY IN HISTORY: The Apostles wait and pray during the last 10 days of the Omer count (Ac. 1:4f). "Do not leave Jerusalem, but wait for the gift my Father promised, which you have heard me speak about…Then they returned to Jerusalem from the hill called the Mount of Olives…They all joined together constantly in prayer" (NIV).

BAMIDBAR (IN THE WILDERNESS)

18 May / 27 Iyar
THURSDAY
DAY 42 OF THE OMER

Numbers 3:14–39 **TORAH** ☐
Jeremiah 10 **PROPHETS** ☐
Job 31 **WRITINGS** ☐
Romans 11 (Matthew 27:32–66) **APOSTLES** ☐

19 May / 28 Iyar
FRIDAY
YOM YERUSHALAYIM
(JERUSALEM DAY)
DAY 43 OF THE OMER

CANDLE LIGHTING TIMES:

TODAY IN HISTORY: Death of Samuel the Prophet (tradition, 1 Sam. 25:1). "Then Samuel died; and all Israel gathered together and mourned for him, and buried him at his house in Ramah." Jerusalem is reunited under Jewish sovereignty during the Six Day War. "This morning, the Israel Defense Forces liberated Jerusalem. We have united Jerusalem, the divided capital of Israel. We have returned to the holiest of our holy places, never to part from it again. To our Arab neighbors we extend, also at this hour…our hand in peace." (Defense Minister Moshe Dayan, June 7, 1967).

BAMIDBAR (IN THE WILDERNESS)

20 May / 29 Iyar

SHABBAT

DAY 44 OF THE OMER

Numbers 4:1–20 **TORAH** ☐
Hosea 1:10–2:20[2:1–22] **HAFTARAH** ☐
1 Corinthians 12:12–27 **APOSTLES** ☐

BAMIDBAR (IN THE WILDERNESS)

□ TORAH	Deuteronomy 14:22–29
	Numbers 28:11–15
□ PROPHETS	Jeremiah 13
□ WRITINGS	Job 33
□ APOSTLES	Romans 13 (Mark 1)

21 May / 1 Sivan

● SUNDAY
ROSH CHODESH
DAY 45 OF THE OMER

TODAY IN HISTORY: The people of Israel arrive in the wilderness of Sinai (Ex. 19:1). "In the third month after the sons of Israel had gone out of the land of Egypt, on that very day they came into the wilderness of Sinai." Korah and his followers perish (tradition, Num. 16:18–50). "…the earth opened its mouth and swallowed them up, and their households, and all the men who belonged to Korah with their possessions." The Prophet Ezekiel receives one of seven prophecies (nearly all dated) against Egypt. "In the eleventh year, in the third month, on the first of the month, the word of the LORD came to me saying, 'Son of man, say to Pharaoh king of Egypt and to his hordes, Whom are you like in your greatness?'" (Eze. 31:1–2).

SHAVUOT (FEAST OF WEEKS)

22 May / 2 Sivan

MONDAY

DAY 46 OF THE OMER

Deuteronomy 15:1–18   **TORAH** ☐

Jeremiah 14   **PROPHETS** ☐

Job 34   **WRITINGS** ☐

Romans 14 (Mark 2)   **APOSTLES** ☐

TODAY IN HISTORY: *Yom HaMeyuchas* (Day of Distinction). The people of Israel are selected as God's chosen people (Ex. 19:4–6). "…if you will indeed obey My voice and keep My covenant, then you shall be My own possession among all the peoples, for all the earth is Mine; and you shall be to Me a kingdom of priests and a holy nation."

SHAVUOT (FEAST OF WEEKS)

☐ **TORAH**	Deuteronomy 15:19–23
☐ **PROPHETS**	Jeremiah 15
☐ **WRITINGS**	Job 35
☐ **APOSTLES**	Romans 15 (Mark 3)

23 May / 3 Sivan
TUESDAY
DAY 47 OF THE OMER

TODAY IN HISTORY: The people of Israel begin three days of preparation for the revelation at Mt. Sinai (Ex. 19:10–12). "Go to the people and consecrate them today and tomorrow, and let them wash their garments; and let them be ready for the third day…You shall set bounds for the people all around [the mountain]…"

SHAVUOT (FEAST OF WEEKS)

24 May / 4 Sivan

WEDNESDAY

DAY 48 OF THE OMER

Deuteronomy 16:1–3   **TORAH** ☐

Jeremiah 16   **PROPHETS** ☐

Job 36   **WRITINGS** ☐

Romans 16 (Mark 4)   **APOSTLES** ☐

TODAY IN HISTORY: Moses writes the first 68 chapters of the Torah (tradition, Ex. 24:4). "Moses wrote down all the words of the LORD."

SHAVUOT (FEAST OF WEEKS)

☐ **TORAH**	Deuteronomy 16:4–8	
☐ **PROPHETS**	Jeremiah 17	
☐ **WRITINGS**	Job 37	
☐ **APOSTLES**	1 Corinthians 1 (Mark 5)	

25 May / 5 Sivan
THURSDAY
SHAVUOT EVE
DAY 49 OF THE OMER

CANDLE LIGHTING TIMES:

TODAY IN HISTORY: The people of Israel say "yes" to the Torah (Ex. 24:7). "Then he took the book of the covenant and read it in the hearing of the people; and they said, 'All that the LORD has spoken we will do, and we will be obedient!'"

SHAVUOT (FEAST OF WEEKS)

26 May / 6 Sivan

FRIDAY
SHAVUOT DAY 1 (FEAST OF WEEKS)

_____

_____

_____

_____

_____

_____

_____

_____

_____

_____

_____

_____

_____

_____

CANDLE LIGHTING TIMES: _____

TODAY IN HISTORY: God gives the Torah on Mt. Sinai (Ex. 19:16–25). "Now Mount Sinai was all in smoke because the LORD descended upon it in fire; and its smoke ascended like the smoke of a furnace, and the whole mountain quaked violently. When the sound of the trumpet grew louder and louder..." Birth and death of King David (tradition, 1 Ki. 2:10). "Then David slept with his fathers and was buried in the city of David." The Spirit of God is poured out on the disciples in the Temple (Ac. 2). "When the [fiftieth day] had come, they were all together in one place. And suddenly there came from heaven a noise like a violent rushing wind, and it filled the whole house where they were sitting."

SHAVUOT (FEAST OF WEEKS) _____

27 May / 7 Sivan
◑ **SHABBAT**
SHAVUOT DAY 2* (FEAST OF WEEKS)

---

* It is customary among the Jewish people, since ancient times, to double the festival sabbath (*yom tov*) outside Israel.

28 May / 8 Sivan
SUNDAY

Numbers 4:21–37 **TORAH** ☐
Jeremiah 18 **PROPHETS** ☐
Job 38 **WRITINGS** ☐
1 Corinthians 2 (Mark 6:1–29) **APOSTLES** ☐

NASSO (TAKE UP)

☐ **TORAH** Numbers 4:38–49
☐ **PROPHETS** Jeremiah 19
☐ **WRITINGS** Job 39
☐ **APOSTLES** 1 Corinthians 3 (Mark 6:30–56)

29 May / 9 Sivan
MONDAY

30 May / 10 Sivan
TUESDAY

NASSO (TAKE UP)

☐ **TORAH** Numbers 5:11–6:27
☐ **PROPHETS** Jeremiah 22
☐ **WRITINGS** Job 41
☐ **APOSTLES** 1 Corinthians 5 (Mark 8)

31 May / 11 Sivan
WEDNESDAY

1 Jun. / 12 Sivan
THURSDAY

Numbers 7:1–41 **TORAH** ☐
Jeremiah 23 **PROPHETS** ☐
Job 42 **WRITINGS** ☐
1 Corinthians 6 (Mark 9:1–29) **APOSTLES** ☐

TODAY IN HISTORY: During the second Temple period this was traditionally the last day sacrifices could be brought after *Shavout* (Feast of Weeks, seven days prior) according to the commandment in Deuteronomy 16:16. "Three times in a year all your males shall appear before the LORD your God in the place which He chooses… and they shall not appear before the LORD empty-handed."

NASSO (TAKE UP)

☐ **TORAH**   Numbers 7:42–71
☐ **PROPHETS**   Jeremiah 24
☐ **WRITINGS**   Daniel 1
☐ **APOSTLES**   1 Corinthians 7 (Mark 9:30–50)

2 Jun. / 13 Sivan
FRIDAY

CANDLE LIGHTING TIMES:

TODAY IN HISTORY: Moses ascends Sinai on the seventh day after God's glory rested on the mountain (tradition, Ex. 24:15–18). "…the cloud covered it for six days; and on the seventh day He called to Moses from the midst of the cloud…Moses entered the midst of the cloud as he went up to the mountain; and Moses was on the mountain forty days and forty nights."

NASSO (TAKE UP)

3 Jun. / 14 Sivan
SHABBAT

Numbers 7:72–89 **TORAH** ☐
Judges 13:2–25 **HAFTARAH** ☐
Acts 21:17–26; 24:14–18 **APOSTLES** ☐

NASSO (TAKE UP)

☐ **TORAH**   Numbers 8:1–14
☐ **PROPHETS**   Jeremiah 25
☐ **WRITINGS**   Daniel 2
☐ **APOSTLES**   1 Corinthians 8 (Mark 10:1–31)

4 Jun. / 15 Sivan
○ SUNDAY

TODAY IN HISTORY: Birth and death of the patriarch Judah (tradition, Gen. 29:35; Ex. 1:6). "And she conceived again and bore a son and said, 'This time I will praise the LORD.' Therefore she named him Judah. Then she stopped bearing."

BEHA'ALOTCHA (WHEN YOU SET UP)

5 Jun. / 16 Sivan
MONDAY

Numbers 8:15–26 **TORAH** ☐
Jeremiah 26 **PROPHETS** ☐
Daniel 3 **WRITINGS** ☐
1 Corinthians 9 (Mark 10:32–52) **APOSTLES** ☐

BEHA'ALOTCHA (WHEN YOU SET UP)

☐ **TORAH**	Numbers 9:1–14	
☐ **PROPHETS**	Jeremiah 27–28	
☐ **WRITINGS**	Daniel 4	
☐ **APOSTLES**	1 Corinthians 10 (Mark 11)	

6 Jun. / 17 Sivan

TUESDAY

BEHA'ALOTCHA (WHEN YOU SET UP)

7 Jun. / 18 Sivan
WEDNESDAY

Numbers 9:15–10:10 **TORAH** ☐
Jeremiah 29 **PROPHETS** ☐
Daniel 5 **WRITINGS** ☐
1 Corinthians 11 (Mark 12) **APOSTLES** ☐

BEHA'ALOTCHA (WHEN YOU SET UP)

☐ **TORAH**	Numbers 10:11–34
☐ **PROPHETS**	Jeremiah 30
☐ **WRITINGS**	Daniel 6
☐ **APOSTLES**	1 Corinthians 12 (Mark 13)

8 Jun. / 19 Sivan
THURSDAY

BEHA'ALOTCHA (WHEN YOU SET UP)

9 Jun. / 20 Sivan
FRIDAY

Numbers 10:35–11:29 **TORAH** ☐
Jeremiah 31 **PROPHETS** ☐
Daniel 7 **WRITINGS** ☐
1 Corinthians 13 (Mark 14:1–42) **APOSTLES** ☐

CANDLE LIGHTING TIMES:

BEHA'ALOTCHA (WHEN YOU SET UP)

11 Jun. / 22 Sivan
SUNDAY

Numbers 13:1–20 **TORAH** ☐
Jeremiah 32 **PROPHETS** ☐
Daniel 8 **WRITINGS** ☐
1 Corinthians 14 (Mark 14:43–72) **APOSTLES** ☐

TODAY IN HISTORY: Miriam punished with *tzara'at*, biblical leprosy (tradition, Num. 12). " 'Why then were you not afraid to speak against My servant, against Moses?'… when the cloud had withdrawn from over the tent, behold, Miriam was leprous, as white as snow… Moses cried out to the LORD, saying, 'O God, heal her, I pray!' "

SHLACH (SEND)

12 Jun. / 23 Sivan
MONDAY

TODAY IN HISTORY: Mordecai writes to everyone in the Medo-Persian Empire concerning the king's decree that the Jews can defend themselves (Est. 8:9). "So the king's scribes were called at that time in the third month (that is, the month Sivan), on the twenty-third day; and it was written according to all that Mordecai commanded to the Jews, the satraps, the governors and the princes of the provinces which extended from India to Ethiopia".

SHLACH (SEND)

13 Jun. / 24 Sivan
TUESDAY

Numbers 14:8–25 **TORAH** ☐
Jeremiah 34 **PROPHETS** ☐
Daniel 10 **WRITINGS** ☐
1 Corinthians 15:29–58 (Mark 16) **APOSTLES** ☐

SHLACH (SEND)

□ **TORAH**   Numbers 14:26–15:7
□ **PROPHETS**   Jeremiah 35
□ **WRITINGS**   Daniel 11:1–20
□ **APOSTLES**   1 Corinthians 16 (Luke 1:1–38)

14 Jun. / 25 Sivan
WEDNESDAY

15 Jun. / 26 Sivan
THURSDAY

SHLACH (SEND)

□ **TORAH**   Numbers 15:17–26
□ **PROPHETS** Jeremiah 37
□ **WRITINGS** Daniel 12
□ **APOSTLES** 2 Corinthians 2 (Luke 2:1–21)

16 Jun. / 27 Sivan
FRIDAY

CANDLE LIGHTING TIMES:

17 Jun. / 28 Sivan
SHABBAT

Numbers 15:27–41   **TORAH** ☐
Joshua 2:1–24   **HAFTARAH** ☐
Hebrews 3:7–4:13   **APOSTLES** ☐

SHLACH (SEND)

□ **TORAH**   Numbers 16:1–13
□ **PROPHETS** Jeremiah 38
□ **WRITINGS** Ezra 1
□ **APOSTLES** 2 Corinthians 3 (Luke 2:22–52)

18 Jun. / 29 Sivan
SUNDAY

TODAY IN HISTORY: The twelve spies are sent to Canaan (tradition, Num. 13:2). "Send out for yourself men so that they may spy out the land of Canaan, which I am going to give to the sons of Israel; you shall send a man from each of their fathers' tribes."

KORACH (KORAH)

19 Jun. / 30 Sivan

MONDAY ●
ROSH CHODESH (DAY 1)

Numbers 16:14–19; 28:11–15   **TORAH** ☐
Jeremiah 39–40   **PROPHETS** ☐
Ezra 2   **WRITINGS** ☐
2 Corinthians 4 (Luke 3)   **APOSTLES** ☐

TODAY IN HISTORY: Death of Christian Zionist pioneer Lt. Col. John Henry Patterson (z"l) year 5707 (1947). Patterson was an Irish Protestant, a British soldier, hunter, and author. His adventures with man-eating lions in Africa inspired several Hollywood films. During WWI, he commanded the Jewish Legion, "the first Jewish fighting force in nearly two millennia." He sacrificed promotion to stand up against significant antisemitism in the military. During WWII, he advocated for a Jewish state and a Jewish army to fight the Nazis and rescue the Jews of Europe, whereupon he lost his military pension. Patterson was close friends with Zionist leaders like Jabotinsky, Trumpeldor, and Benzion Netanyahu. In 2014, 67 years after his death, he and his wife were reinterred in Israel. At the burial, PM Benjamin Netanyahu, whose older brother (Yonatan) was named after Patterson, called him "the godfather of the IDF."

KORACH (KORAH)

TODAY IN HISTORY: Birth and death of the patriarch Joseph (tradition, Gen. 30:23, 50:26). "So she [Rachel] conceived and bore a son and said, 'God has taken away my reproach.' She named him Joseph, saying, 'May the LORD give me another son'… So Joseph died at the age of one hundred and ten years; and he was embalmed and placed in a coffin in Egypt."

KORACH (KORAH)

21 Jun. / 2 Tamuz
WEDNESDAY

Numbers 16:44–50[17:9–15]   **TORAH** ☐
Jeremiah 42–43   **PROPHETS** ☐
Ezra 4   **WRITINGS** ☐
2 Corinthians 6 (Luke 5)   **APOSTLES** ☐

KORACH (KORAH)

22 Jun. / 3 Tamuz
THURSDAY

TODAY IN HISTORY: Joshua commands the sun and moon to stand still (tradition, Jos. 10: 11–14). "So the sun stood still, and the moon stopped… There was no day like that before it or after it, when the LORD listened to the voice of a man; for the LORD fought for Israel."

KORACH (KORAH)

23 Jun. / 4 Tamuz
FRIDAY

CANDLE LIGHTING TIMES:

KORACH (KORAH)

TODAY IN HISTORY: The Prophet Ezekiel sees a vision of the "*Merkava*" (Chariot) of God (Eze. 1). "Now it came about in the thirtieth year, on the fifth day of the fourth month, while I was by the river Chebar among the exiles, the heavens were opened and I saw visions of God."

KORACH (KORAH)

25 Jun. / 6 Tamuz
SUNDAY

Numbers 19:1–20:6   **TORAH** ☐
Jeremiah 48   **PROPHETS** ☐
Ezra 7   **WRITINGS** ☐
2 Corinthians 9 (Luke 7:1–23)   **APOSTLES** ☐

CHUKAT (STATUTE) / BALAK (BALAK)

26 Jun. / 7 Tamuz

◐ MONDAY

27 Jun. / 8 Tamuz
TUESDAY

Numbers 20:22–21:20   **TORAH** ☐
Jeremiah 50   **PROPHETS** ☐
Ezra 9   **WRITINGS** ☐
2 Corinthians 11 (Luke 8:1–25)   **APOSTLES** ☐

CHUKAT (STATUTE) / BALAK (BALAK)

☐ **TORAH**	Numbers 21:21–22:12	
☐ **PROPHETS**	Jeremiah 51	
☐ **WRITINGS**	Ezra 10	
☐ **APOSTLES**	2 Corinthians 12 (Luke 8:26–56)	

28 Jun. / 9 Tamuz
WEDNESDAY

TODAY IN HISTORY: The Babylonians break through the walls of Jerusalem (Jer. 39:2, 2 Ki. 25:1f). "…in the fourth month, in the ninth day of the month, the city wall was breached. Then all the officials of the king of Babylon came in and sat down at the Middle Gate." The 9th of Tamuz was originally a fast day, but was moved after the Romans broke through the walls on the 17th of Tamuz (70 CE).

CHUKAT (STATUTE) / BALAK (BALAK)

29 Jun. / 10 Tamuz
THURSDAY

Numbers 22:13–38 **TORAH** ☐
Jeremiah 52 **PROPHETS** ☐
Nehemiah 1 **WRITINGS** ☐
2 Corinthians 13 (Luke 9:1–26) **APOSTLES** ☐

CHUKAT (STATUTE) / BALAK (BALAK)

☐ **TORAH**   Numbers 22:39–23:26
☐ **PROPHETS** Ezekiel 1
☐ **WRITINGS** Nehemiah 2
☐ **APOSTLES** Galatians 1 (Luke 9:27–62)

30 Jun. / 11 Tamuz
FRIDAY

CANDLE LIGHTING TIMES:

CHUKAT (STATUTE) / BALAK (BALAK)

1 Jul. / 12 Tamuz
SHABBAT

Numbers 23:27–25:9   **TORAH** ☐

Micah 5:7[6]–6:8   **HAFTARAH** ☐

2 Peter 2   **APOSTLES** ☐

CHUKAT (STATUTE) / BALAK (BALAK)

3 Jul. / 14 Tamuz
MONDAY ○

Numbers 26:5–51 **TORAH** ☐
Ezekiel 4–5 **PROPHETS** ☐
Nehemiah 4 **WRITINGS** ☐
Galatians 3 (Luke 11:1–28) **APOSTLES** ☐

PINCHAS (PHINEHAS)

TORAH	Numbers 26:52–27:5
PROPHETS	Ezekiel 6–7
WRITINGS	Nehemiah 5
APOSTLES	Galatians 4 (Luke 11:29–54)

4 Jul. / 15 Tamuz

TUESDAY

5 Jul. / 16 Tamuz
WEDNESDAY

TODAY IN HISTORY: The golden calf is made (tradition, Ex. 32:1–5). "Now when the people saw that Moses delayed to come down from the mountain, the people assembled about Aaron and said to him, 'Come, make us a god who will go before us; as for this Moses, the man who brought us up from the land of Egypt, we do not know what has become of him.'"

PINCHAS (PHINEHAS)

☐ **TORAH**   Numbers 28:1–15
☐ **PROPHETS**   Ezekiel 10–11
☐ **WRITINGS**   Nehemiah 7
☐ **APOSTLES**   Galatians 6 (Luke 12:35–59)
☐ **SYNAGOGUE READINGS**
Exodus 32:11–14; 34:1–10; Isaiah 55:6–56:8 (afternoon)

6 Jul. / 17 Tamuz
THURSDAY
FAST OF TAMUZ

TODAY IN HISTORY: The fast of the fourth month (Zec. 8:19). "Thus says the LORD of hosts, 'The fast of the fourth, the fast of the fifth, the fast of the seventh and the fast of the tenth months will become joy, gladness, and cheerful feasts for the house of Judah.'"   Moses breaks the stone tablets (tradition, Ex. 32:6–19). "It came about, as soon as Moses came near the camp, that he saw the calf and the dancing; and Moses' anger burned, and he threw the tablets from his hands and shattered them at the foot of the mountain."   Moses destroys the golden calf (tradition, Ex. 32:20–35). "He took the calf which they had made and burned it with fire, and ground it to powder, and scattered it over the surface of the water and made the sons of Israel drink it."   The daily sacrifice in the Temple ceases because of the Babylonian siege year 586 BCE (tradition).   The Romans break through the walls of Jerusalem year 70 CE (tradition).   The Fast of Tamuz is a shorter fast on the Jewish calendar and lasts from sunrise to sunset. It is one of four similar, biblical fast days. Normally observed on the 17th of Tamuz, it may be moved if its observance would conflict with Shabbat.   *Bein HaMetzarim* (the time "between the straits") begins—the three weeks of mourning leading up to the 9th of Av.

PINCHAS (PHINEHAS)

7 Jul. / 18 Tamuz
FRIDAY

CANDLE LIGHTING TIMES:

PINCHAS (PHINEHAS)

After the Fast of Tamuz and for the next ten Sabbaths, the *Haftarah* (the reading from the Prophets) no longer corresponds specifically to the Torah portion, but is determined entirely by the time of year and the corresponding historical events. The reading from Jeremiah 1:1–2:3 during the "three weeks" of mourning, begins the three "*Haftarot* of reproof," followed by seven "*Haftarot* of consolation" leading up to *Rosh HaShanah* (Trumpets).

PINCHAS (PHINEHAS)

9 Jul. / 20 Tamuz
SUNDAY

Numbers 30:1[2]–31:12 **TORAH** ☐
Ezekiel 14–15 **PROPHETS** ☐
Nehemiah 9 **WRITINGS** ☐
Ephesians 2 (Luke 14) **APOSTLES** ☐

MATTOT (TRIBES) / MASSEI (JOURNEYS)

10 Jul. / 21 Tamuz
◑ MONDAY

11 Jul. / 22 Tamuz
TUESDAY

MATTOT (TRIBES) / MASSEI (JOURNEYS)

☐ **TORAH**	Numbers 32:20–33:49	
☐ **PROPHETS**	Ezekiel 17	
☐ **WRITINGS**	Nehemiah 12	
☐ **APOSTLES**	Ephesians 5 (Luke 17)	

12 Jul. / 23 Tamuz
WEDNESDAY

13 Jul. / 24 Tamuz
THURSDAY

MATTOT (TRIBES) / MASSEI (JOURNEYS)

☐ **TORAH** Numbers 34:16–35:8
☐ **PROPHETS** Ezekiel 20
☐ **WRITINGS** 1 Chronicles 1
☐ **APOSTLES** Philippians 1 (Luke 19)

14 Jul. / 25 Tamuz
FRIDAY

CANDLE LIGHTING TIMES:

MATTOT (TRIBES) / MASSEI (JOURNEYS)

15 Jul. / 26 Tamuz
SHABBAT

Numbers 35:9–36:13   **TORAH** ☐
Jeremiah 2:4–28; 3:4 **HAFTARAH** ☐
James 4:1–12 **APOSTLES** ☐

MATTOT (TRIBES) / MASSEI (JOURNEYS)

☐ **TORAH** Deuteronomy 1:1–10
☐ **PROPHETS** Ezekiel 21
☐ **WRITINGS** 1 Chronicles 2
☐ **APOSTLES** Philippians 2 (Luke 20)

16 Jul. / 27 Tamuz
SUNDAY

17 Jul. / 28 Tamuz
MONDAY

Deuteronomy 1:11–21 **TORAH** ☐
Ezekiel 22 **PROPHETS** ☐
1 Chronicles 3 **WRITINGS** ☐
Philippians 3 (Luke 21) **APOSTLES** ☐

DVARIM (WORDS)

☐ **TORAH**   Deuteronomy 1:22–1:38
☐ **PROPHETS**   Ezekiel 23
☐ **WRITINGS**   1 Chronicles 4
☐ **APOSTLES**   Philippians 4 (Luke 22:1–38)

18 Jul. / 29 Tamuz
TUESDAY

TODAY IN HISTORY: The Apostle Shaul, Paul of Tarsus, is martyred in Rome (tradition, *Book of the Bee* 48). Tradition holds that he was beheaded (Roman citizens were not crucified) during the reign of Nero, following the great fire in the city in 64 CE. "…the time of my departure has come. I have fought the good fight, I have finished the course, I have kept the faith" (2 Tim. 4:6–7).

It's time to order the new

DAILY BREAD
5784 / 2023-2024

for next year!

Go to:
arielmedia.shop

Get a special discount when you use the
following Promo Code:
NEXTYEAR
Valid until 31 Aug. 2023

ARIEL MEDIA   ARIELMEDIA.SHOP

☐ **TORAH**	Deuteronomy 1:39–2:1
	Numbers 28:11–15
☐ **PROPHETS**	Ezekiel 24–25
☐ **WRITINGS**	1 Chronicles 5
☐ **APOSTLES**	Colossians 1 (Luke 22:39–71)

19 Jul. / 1 Av
● WEDNESDAY
ROSH CHODESH

TODAY IN HISTORY: Death of Aaron, the brother of Moses (Num. 33:38). "Then Aaron the priest went up to Mount Hor at the command of the LORD, and died there in the fortieth year after the sons of Israel had come from the land of Egypt, on the first day in the fifth month." Ezra the Scribe arrives in Jerusalem (Ezr. 7:1–9). "…on the first of the fifth month he came to Jerusalem, because the good hand of his God was upon him." Death of Messianic pioneer Rabbi Paul Feivel Levertoff (zt"l) year 5714 (1954 CE). Feivel Levertoff was born into an orthodox Jewish family with Chasidic ancestry in Orsha, Belarus. After graduating from the prestigious Volozhin Yeshiva in Lithuania, he became a believer in Yeshua of Nazareth. He spent the rest of his life laboring toward the formation of Jewish Christianity, a forerunner of the modern Messianic Jewish movement (vineofdavid.org). The last and more intense days of mourning begin up until the 9th of Av.

20 Jul. / 2 Av
THURSDAY

Deuteronomy 2:2–30   **TORAH** ☐
Ezekiel 26   **PROPHETS** ☐
1 Chronicles 6   **WRITINGS** ☐
Colossians 2 (Luke 23:1–25)   **APOSTLES** ☐

DVARIM (WORDS)

☐ **TORAH**   Deuteronomy 2:31–3:14
☐ **PROPHETS**   Ezekiel 27
☐ **WRITINGS**   1 Chronicles 7
☐ **APOSTLES**   Colossians 3 (Luke 23:26–56)

21 Jul. / 3 Av
FRIDAY

CANDLE LIGHTING TIMES:

DVARIM (WORDS)

22 Jul. / 4 Av

SHABBAT CHAZON
(SABBATH OF VISION)

Deuteronomy 3:15–22   **TORAH** ☐

Isaiah 1:1–27   **HAFTARAH** ☐

Matthew 3:1–12   **APOSTLES** ☐

TODAY IN HISTORY: *Shabbat Chazon* (Sabbath of Vision) is the Sabbath immediately prior to the Fast of the Ninth of Av, the third of the three Sabbaths of reproof, and is the "saddest" Sabbath of the year. It takes its name from the *Haftarah* (prophetic portion) read from Isaiah 1:1–27. "The vision [*chazon*] of Isaiah the son of Amoz concerning Judah and Jerusalem… 'Sons I have reared and brought up, But they have revolted against Me.'"

DVARIM (WORDS)

☐ **TORAH**	Deuteronomy 3:23–4:4
☐ **PROPHETS**	Ezekiel 28
☐ **WRITINGS**	1 Chronicles 8
☐ **APOSTLES**	Colossians 4 (Luke 24)

23 Jul. / 5 Av
SUNDAY

VA'ETCHANAN (AND I PLEADED)

24 Jul. / 6 Av
MONDAY

Deuteronomy 4:5–40 **TORAH** ☐
Ezekiel 29 **PROPHETS** ☐
1 Chronicles 9 **WRITINGS** ☐
1 Thessalonians 1 (John 1:1–28) **APOSTLES** ☐

VA'ETCHANAN (AND I PLEADED)

☐ **TORAH**   Deuteronomy 4:41–49
☐ **PROPHETS**   Ezekiel 30
☐ **WRITINGS**   1 Chronicles 10
☐ **APOSTLES**   1 Thessalonians 2 (John 1:29–51)

25 Jul. / 7 Av
TUESDAY

TODAY IN HISTORY: The Babylonians lay siege to the first Temple (2 Ki. 25:8). "Now on the seventh day of the fifth month, which was the nineteenth year of King Nebuchadnezzar, king of Babylon, Nebuzaradan the captain of the guard, a servant of the king of Babylon, came to Jerusalem."

VA'ETCHANAN (AND I PLEADED)

26 Jul. / 8 Av

WEDNESDAY ◑
EVE OF THE FAST OF AV

Deuteronomy 5:1–21[18]   **TORAH** ☐
Ezekiel 31   **PROPHETS** ☐
1 Chronicles 11   **WRITINGS** ☐
1 Thessalonians 3 (John 2)   **APOSTLES** ☐

TODAY IN HISTORY: The twelve spies return from Canaan (Num. 13:25–33). When they returned from spying out the land, at the end of forty days…they gave out to the sons of Israel a bad report of the land which they had spied out…" Civil war breaks out in Jerusalem year 67 CE (tradition).

VA'ETCHANAN (AND I PLEADED)

☐ **WRITINGS**	**Book of Lamentations** 1–5 (evening)	
☐ **TORAH**	Deuteronomy 4:25–40 (morning)	
☐ **PROPHETS**	Jeremiah 8:13–9:23 (morning)	
☐ **APOSTLES**	1 Corinthians 3:1–20 (Messianic, morning)	
☐ **TORAH**	Exodus 32:11–14; 34:10 (afternoon)	
☐ **PROPHETS**	Isaiah 55:6–56:8 (afternoon)	
☐ **APOSTLES**	Matthew 5:1–12 (Messianic, afternoon)	

27 Jul. / 9 Av
THURSDAY
FAST OF AV

TODAY IN HISTORY: The fast of the fifth month (Zec. 7:3f, 8:19). The Ninth of Av (*Tisha B'Av*) is the most serious fast day on the Jewish calendar besides *Yom Kippur* and lasts from sunset to sunset. It is one of four similar biblical fast days mentioned by the Prophets. It may be moved if its observance would conflict with Shabbat. The generation in the wilderness is condemned to wander for 40 years and die in the wilderness (tradition, Num. 14). "'As I live,' says the LORD, 'just as you have spoken in My hearing, so I will surely do to you; your corpses will fall in this wilderness, even all your numbered men, according to your complete number from twenty years old and upward." The first Temple is destroyed by the Babylonians year 586 BCE (tradition, 2 Ki. 25:9). The second Temple is destroyed by the Romans year 70 CE (tradition). "As he approached Jerusalem and saw the city, he wept over it and said, '...They will dash you to the ground, you and the children within your walls. They will not leave one stone on another'" (Lk. 19:41,44 NIV). The Bar Kochba revolt is crushed by the Romans at Beitar (133 CE). The Jews are expelled from England by King Edward I (1290 CE). The Jews are expelled from Spain by King Ferdinand och Queen Isabella (1492 CE). The Nazis begin the mass deportation of Jews from the Warsaw Ghetto, en route to Treblinka death camp (1942 CE).

VA'ETCHANAN (AND I PLEADED)

28 Jul. / 10 Av
FRIDAY

Deuteronomy 5:22[19]–6:3   **TORAH** ☐
Ezekiel 32   **PROPHETS** ☐
1 Chronicles 12   **WRITINGS** ☐
1 Thessalonians 4 (John 3)   **APOSTLES** ☐

CANDLE LIGHTING TIMES: _____

TODAY IN HISTORY: The Prophet Ezekiel receives a rebuke to certain elders of Israel in exile (Eze. 20). "Now in the seventh year, in the fifth month, on the tenth of the month, certain of the elders of Israel came to inquire of the LORD, and sat before me." Nebuzaradan burns the first Temple (Jer. 52:12f). "Now on the tenth day of the fifth month…Nebuzaradan the captain of the bodyguard, who was in the service of the king of Babylon, came to Jerusalem. He burned the house of the LORD, the king's house and all the houses of Jerusalem; even every large house he burned with fire." The second Temple continues to burn (tradition, 70 CE). Israeli security forces commence forcibly expelling circa 9,000 Jews from their homes in Gush Katif and the other Jewish communities of Gaza, as part of Prime Minister Ariel Sharon's plan of unilateral disengagement (August 15, 2005). *Bein HaMetzarim* (the time "between the straits") ends—the three weeks of mourning from the 17th of Tamuz to the 9th of Av.

VA'ETCHANAN (AND I PLEADED)

☐ **TORAH**   Deuteronomy 6:4–7:11
☐ **HAFTARAH** Isaiah 40:1–26
☐ **APOSTLES**   1 Peter 1:18–25

29 Jul. / 11 Av
SHABBAT NACHAMU
(SABBATH OF CONSOLATION)

TODAY IN HISTORY: *Shabbat Nachamu* (Sabbath of Consolation) is the Sabbath immediately following the Ninth of Av and is the first of the seven "*Haftarot* (prophetic portions) of Consolation" leading up to *Rosh HaShanah* (Trumpets). *Shabbat Nachamu* gets its name from the *Haftarah* of Isaiah 40:1–26, "Comfort, O comfort My people [*Nachamu, nachamu ami*]."

VA'ETCHANAN (AND I PLEADED)

30 Jul. / 12 Av
SUNDAY

Deuteronomy 7:12–8:10   **TORAH** ☐
Ezekiel 33   **PROPHETS** ☐
1 Chronicles 13   **WRITINGS** ☐
1 Thessalonians 5 (John 4:1–30)   **APOSTLES** ☐

EKEV (CONSEQUENCE)

☐ **TORAH**	Deuteronomy 8:11–9:3
☐ **PROPHETS**	Ezekiel 34–35
☐ **WRITINGS**	1 Chronicles 14
☐ **APOSTLES**	2 Thessalonians 1 (John 4:31–54)

31 Jul. / 13 Av
MONDAY

1 Aug. / 14 Av
TUESDAY ○

EKEV (CONSEQUENCE)

TODAY IN HISTORY: *Tu B'Av*, the 15th of Av is *Chag HaAhavah* (Festival of Love). In ancient times, the annual ingathering of wood for the Temple altar was concluded and celebrated as the 'day of the breaking of the ax.' The daughters of Jerusalem would go out to dance in the vineyards and whoever was not married would go there to find a bride (tradition, *b.Taanit* 31a).

3 Aug. / 16 Av
THURSDAY

EKEV (CONSEQUENCE)

□ **TORAH**   Deuteronomy 11:10–21

□ **PROPHETS**   Ezekiel 39

□ **WRITINGS**   1 Chronicles 18

□ **APOSTLES**   1 Timothy 2 (John 7)

4 Aug. / 17 Av

FRIDAY

CANDLE LIGHTING TIMES:

EKEV (CONSEQUENCE)

5 Aug. / 18 Av
SHABBAT

Deuteronomy 11:22–25   **TORAH** ☐
Isaiah 49:14–51:3   **HAFTARAH** ☐
James 5:7–11   **APOSTLES** ☐

EKEV (CONSEQUENCE)

☐ **TORAH**	Deuteronomy 11:26–12:10
☐ **PROPHETS**	Ezekiel 40
☐ **WRITINGS**	1 Chronicles 19
☐ **APOSTLES**	1 Timothy 3 (John 8:1–30)

6 Aug. / 19 Av
SUNDAY

RE'EH (SEE)

7 Aug. / 20 Av
MONDAY

RE'EH (SEE)

□ **TORAH**	Deuteronomy 12:29–13:18[19]
□ **PROPHETS**	Ezekiel 42
□ **WRITINGS**	1 Chronicles 21
□ **APOSTLES**	1 Timothy 5 (John 9)

8 Aug. / 21 Av

◑ TUESDAY

9 Aug. / 22 Av
WEDNESDAY ◑

Deuteronomy 14:1–21   **TORAH** ☐
Ezekiel 43   **PROPHETS** ☐
1 Chronicles 22   **WRITINGS** ☐
1 Timothy 6 (John 10)   **APOSTLES** ☐

RE'EH (SEE)

☐ **TORAH** Deuteronomy 14:22–29
☐ **PROPHETS** Ezekiel 44
☐ **WRITINGS** 1 Chronicles 23
☐ **APOSTLES** 2 Timothy 1 (John 11:1–27)

10 Aug. / 23 Av
THURSDAY

11 Aug. / 24 Av
FRIDAY

Deuteronomy 15:1–18 **TORAH** ☐
Ezekiel 45 **PROPHETS** ☐
1 Chronicles 24 **WRITINGS** ☐
2 Timothy 2 (John 11:28–57) **APOSTLES** ☐

CANDLE LIGHTING TIMES:

RE'EH (SEE)

☐ **TORAH** Deuteronomy 15:19–16:17
☐ **HAFTARAH** Isaiah 54:11–55:5
☐ **APOSTLES** Revelation 21:9–27

12 Aug. / 25 Av
SHABBAT

RE'EH (SEE)

13 Aug. / 26 Av
SUNDAY

Deuteronomy 16:18–17:13   **TORAH** ☐
Ezekiel 46   **PROPHETS** ☐
1 Chronicles 25   **WRITINGS** ☐
2 Timothy 3 (John 12:1–19)   **APOSTLES** ☐

SHOFTIM (JUDGES)

☐ **TORAH** Deuteronomy 17:14–20
☐ **PROPHETS** Ezekiel 47
☐ **WRITINGS** 1 Chronicles 26
☐ **APOSTLES** 2 Timothy 4 (John 12:20–50)

14 Aug. / 27 Av
MONDAY

SHOFTIM (JUDGES)

15 Aug. / 28 Av
TUESDAY

Deuteronomy 18:1–5   **TORAH** ☐
Ezekiel 48   **PROPHETS** ☐
1 Chronicles 27   **WRITINGS** ☐
Titus 1 (John 13)   **APOSTLES** ☐

SHOFTIM (JUDGES)

☐ **TORAH**   Deuteronomy 18:6–13
☐ **PROPHETS**   Hosea 1–2
☐ **WRITINGS**   1 Chronicles 28
☐ **APOSTLES**   Titus 2 (John 14)

16 Aug. / 29 Av
WEDNESDAY

17 Aug. / 30 Av

THURSDAY ●
ROSH CHODESH (DAY 1)
DAY 1 OF REPENTANCE

Deuteronomy 18:14–19:13   **TORAH** ☐
Numbers 28:11–15
Hosea 3–4   **PROPHETS** ☐
1 Chronicles 29   **WRITINGS** ☐
Titus 3 (John 15)   **APOSTLES** ☐

TODAY IN HISTORY: Moses carves out new stone tablets (tradition, Ex. 34:1f). "Now the LORD said to Moses, 'Cut out for yourself two stone tablets like the former ones, and I will write on the tablets the words that were on the former tablets which you shattered.'"

SHOFTIM (JUDGES)

☐ **TORAH**	Deuteronomy 19:14–20:9
	Numbers 28:11–15
☐ **PROPHETS**	Hosea 5–6
☐ **WRITINGS**	2 Chronicles 1
☐ **APOSTLES**	Philemon (John 16)

18 Aug. / 1 Elul
● FRIDAY
ROSH CHODESH (DAY 2)
DAY 2 OF REPENTANCE

CANDLE LIGHTING TIMES:

TODAY IN HISTORY: Moses ascends Mt. Sinai a second time (tradition, Ex. 33:18–34:28). "…
Moses rose up early in the morning and went up to Mount Sinai, as the LORD had commanded him, and he took two stone tablets in his hand." The Prophet Haggai receives a
prophecy to rebuild the Temple (Hag. 1). "In the second year of Darius the king, on the first
day of the sixth month, the word of the LORD came by the prophet Haggai…'Is it time for you
yourselves to dwell in your paneled houses while this house lies desolate?'" Possible beginning of Messiah's 40-day fast in the wilderness (Mt. 4:1, Mk. 1:12, Lk. 4:1). "Yeshua, full of the Holy
Spirit, returned from the Jordan and was led around by the Spirit in the wilderness…" *Rosh
Hashana LaBehemot* (New Year for Animals). In the Torah, God instructs that a tithe of all ko-
sher domesticated animals be sanctified to the Temple (Lev 27:32–33). In Temple times, the
New Year for Animals was the day shepherds determined which animals were to be tithed.

SHOFTIM (JUDGES)

19 Aug. / 2 Elul

SHABBAT

DAY 3 OF REPENTANCE

Deuteronomy 20:10–21:9   **TORAH** ☐
Isaiah 51:12–52:12 **HAFTARAH** ☐
2 Thessalonians 1 **APOSTLES** ☐

☐ **TORAH**   Deuteronomy 21:10–21
☐ **PROPHETS**   Hosea 7–8
☐ **WRITINGS**   2 Chronicles 2
☐ **APOSTLES**   Hebrews 1 (John 17)

20 Aug. / 3 Elul
SUNDAY
DAY 4 OF REPENTANCE

21 Aug. / 4 Elul

MONDAY

DAY 5 OF REPENTANCE

Deuteronomy 21:22–22:7 **TORAH** ☐

Hosea 9–10 **PROPHETS** ☐

2 Chronicles 3 **WRITINGS** ☐

Hebrews 2 (John 18) **APOSTLES** ☐

KI TETZE (WHEN YOU GO OUT)

☐ **TORAH**	Deuteronomy 22:8–23:6[7]
☐ **PROPHETS**	Hosea 11–12
☐ **WRITINGS**	2 Chronicles 4
☐ **APOSTLES**	Hebrews 3 (John 19)

22 Aug. / 5 Elul
TUESDAY
DAY 6 OF REPENTANCE

TODAY IN HISTORY: The Prophet Ezekiel sees a vision of abominations in the Temple (Eze. 8). "It came about in the sixth year, on the fifth day of the sixth month, as I was sitting in my house with the elders of Judah sitting before me, that the hand of the Lord GOD fell on me there…and the Spirit lifted me up between earth and heaven and brought me in the visions of God to Jerusalem."

KI TETZE (WHEN YOU GO OUT)

23 Aug. / 6 Elul

WEDNESDAY

DAY 7 OF REPENTANCE

Deuteronomy 23:7–23[8–24]   **TORAH** ☐

Hosea 13–14   **PROPHETS** ☐

2 Chronicles 5   **WRITINGS** ☐

Hebrews 4 (John 20)   **APOSTLES** ☐

KI TETZE (WHEN YOU GO OUT)

□ **TORAH**   Deuteronomy 23:24[25]–24:4
□ **PROPHETS** Joel 1
□ **WRITINGS** 2 Chronicles 6:1–21
□ **APOSTLES** Hebrews 5 (John 21)

24 Aug. / 7 Elul
◗ THURSDAY
DAY 8 OF REPENTANCE

TODAY IN HISTORY: Death of the ten spies who gave the bad report (tradition, Num. 14). "As for the men whom Moses sent to spy out the land and who returned and made all the congregation grumble against him by bringing out a bad report concerning the land…died by a plague before the LORD."

KI TETZE (WHEN YOU GO OUT)

25 Aug. / 8 Elul

FRIDAY

DAY 9 OF REPENTANCE

Deuteronomy 24:5–13   **TORAH** ☐

Joel 2 [2–3]   **PROPHETS** ☐

2 Chronicles 6:22–42   **WRITINGS** ☐

Hebrews 6 (Acts 1)   **APOSTLES** ☐

CANDLE LIGHTING TIMES:

KI TETZE (WHEN YOU GO OUT)

26 Aug. / 9 Elul
SHABBAT
DAY 10 OF REPENTANCE

KI TETZE (WHEN YOU GO OUT)

27 Aug. / 10 Elul

SUNDAY

DAY 11 OF REPENTANCE

Deuteronomy 26:1–11   **TORAH** ☐

Joel 3 [4]   **PROPHETS** ☐

2 Chronicles 7   **WRITINGS** ☐

Hebrews 7 (Acts 2)   **APOSTLES** ☐

KI TAVO (WHEN YOU COME IN)

☐ **TORAH** Deuteronomy 26:12–15
☐ **PROPHETS** Amos 1–2
☐ **WRITINGS** 2 Chronicles 8
☐ **APOSTLES** Hebrews 8 (Acts 3)

28 Aug. / 11 Elul
MONDAY
DAY 12 OF REPENTANCE

29 Aug. / 12 Elul

TUESDAY

DAY 13 OF REPENTANCE

Deuteronomy 26:16–19   **TORAH** ☐

Amos 3–4   **PROPHETS** ☐

2 Chronicles 9   **WRITINGS** ☐

Hebrews 9 (Acts 4)   **APOSTLES** ☐

KI TAVO (WHEN YOU COME IN)

□ **TORAH**   Deuteronomy 27:1–10
□ **PROPHETS**   Amos 5
□ **WRITINGS**   2 Chronicles 10
□ **APOSTLES**   Hebrews 10 (Acts 5)

30 Aug. / 13 Elul
WEDNESDAY
DAY 14 OF REPENTANCE

KI TAVO (WHEN YOU COME IN)

31 Aug. / 14 Elul
THURSDAY ○
DAY 15 OF REPENTANCE

Deuteronomy 27:11–28:6   **TORAH** ☐
Amos 6–7   **PROPHETS** ☐
2 Chronicles 11   **WRITINGS** ☐
Hebrews 11:1–19 (Acts 6)   **APOSTLES** ☐

KI TAVO (WHEN YOU COME IN)

☐ **TORAH** Deuteronomy 28:7–29:1[28:69]
☐ **PROPHETS** Amos 8–9
☐ **WRITINGS** 2 Chronicles 12
☐ **APOSTLES** Hebrews 11:20–40 (Acts 7:1–29)

1 Sep. / 15 Elul
FRIDAY
DAY 16 OF REPENTANCE

CANDLE LIGHTING TIMES:

KI TAVO (WHEN YOU COME IN)

2 Sep. / 16 Elul

SHABBAT

DAY 17 OF REPENTANCE

Deuteronomy 29:2–9[1–8]   **TORAH** ☐
Isaiah 60:1–22   **HAFTARAH** ☐
Romans 8:31–39   **APOSTLES** ☐

KI TAVO (WHEN YOU COME IN)

☐ TORAH	Deuteronomy 29:10–29[9–28]
☐ PROPHETS	Obadiah 1
☐ WRITINGS	2 Chronicles 13
☐ APOSTLES	Hebrews 12 (Acts 7:30–60)

3 Sep. / 17 Elul

SUNDAY
DAY 18 OF REPENTANCE

4 Sep. / 18 Elul

MONDAY

DAY 19 OF REPENTANCE

Deuteronomy 30:1–6   **TORAH** ☐

Micah 1–2   **PROPHETS** ☐

2 Chronicles 14   **WRITINGS** ☐

Hebrews 13 (Acts 8)   **APOSTLES** ☐

NITZAVIM (STANDING) / VAYELECH (AND HE WENT)

☐ TORAH	Deuteronomy 30:7–14
☐ PROPHETS	Micah 3–4
☐ WRITINGS	2 Chronicles 15
☐ APOSTLES	Revelation 1 (Acts 9)

5 Sep. / 19 Elul
TUESDAY
DAY 20 OF REPENTANCE

6 Sep. / 20 Elul
WEDNESDAY
DAY 21 OF REPENTANCE

Deuteronomy 30:15–31:6 **TORAH** ☐
Micah 5 **PROPHETS** ☐
2 Chronicles 16 **WRITINGS** ☐
Revelation 2:1–17 (Acts 10) **APOSTLES** ☐

NITZAVIM (STANDING) / VAYELECH (AND HE WENT)

☐ **TORAH** Deuteronomy 31:7–13

☐ **PROPHETS** Micah 6

☐ **WRITINGS** 2 Chronicles 17

☐ **APOSTLES** Revelation 2:18–29 (Acts 11)

7 Sep. / 21 Elul

◑ THURSDAY

DAY 22 OF REPENTANCE

8 Sep. / 22 Elul

FRIDAY

DAY 23 OF REPENTANCE

Deuteronomy 31:14–19   TORAH ☐

Micah 7   PROPHETS ☐

2 Chronicles 18   WRITINGS ☐

Revelation 3 (Acts 12)   APOSTLES ☐

CANDLE LIGHTING TIMES:

NITZAVIM (STANDING) / VAYELECH (AND HE WENT)

☐ **TORAH**   Deuteronomy 31:20–30
☐ **HAFTARAH**   Isaiah 61:10–63:9
☐ **APOSTLES**   Luke 4:14–21

9 Sep. / 23 Elul
SHABBAT
LEIL SLICHOT
DAY 24 OF REPENTANCE

Leil Slichot (Night of Repentance Prayers): *Slichot* are penitential prayers and poems, especially those said in the period leading up to the High Holidays, and on Fast Days. In the Ashkenazi tradition, *Leil Slichot* begins on the Saturday night before Rosh Hashanah. If, however, the first day of *Rosh Hashanah* falls on Monday or Tuesday, *Slichot* are said beginning the previous Saturday night. In Sephardic tradition, *Slichot* begin on the 2nd of Elul.

NITZAVIM (STANDING) / VAYELECH (AND HE WENT)

10 Sep. / 24 Elul

SUNDAY

DAY 25 OF REPENTANCE

TODAY IN HISTORY: Zerubbabel, Joshua the High Priest, and the people of Israel resume building the second Temple (Hag. 1:14f). "So the LORD stirred up the spirit of Zerubbabel the son of Shealtiel, governor of Judah, and the spirit of Joshua the son of Jehozadak, the high priest, and the spirit of all the remnant of the people; and they came and worked on the house of the LORD of hosts, their God, on the twenty-fourth day of the sixth month in the second year of Darius the king."

ROSH HASHANAH (FEAST OF TRUMPETS)

☐ **TORAH** Genesis 21:5–8
☐ **PROPHETS** Nahum 3
☐ **WRITINGS** 2 Chronicles 20:1–19
☐ **APOSTLES** Revelation 5 (Acts 13:26–52)

11 Sep. / 25 Elul
MONDAY
DAY 26 OF REPENTANCE

TODAY IN HISTORY: The first day of creation, six days before the traditional date of the creation of man on *Rosh HaShanah* (Feast of Trumpets, Gen. 1:1–5). "Then God said, 'Let there be light'; and there was light…And there was evening and there was morning, one day."   The rebuilding of Jerusalem's walls is completed (Neh. 6:15). "So the wall was completed on the twenty-fifth of the month Elul, in fifty-two days."

ROSH HASHANAH (FEAST OF TRUMPETS)

12 Sep. / 26 Elul

TUESDAY

DAY 27 OF REPENTANCE

Genesis 21:9–12	**TORAH** ☐
Habakkuk 1–2	**PROPHETS** ☐
2 Chronicles 20:20–37	**WRITINGS** ☐
Revelation 6 (Acts 14)	**APOSTLES** ☐

ROSH HASHANAH (FEAST OF TRUMPETS)

☐ **TORAH**	Genesis 21:13–17
☐ **PROPHETS**	Habakkuk 3
☐ **WRITINGS**	2 Chronicles 21
☐ **APOSTLES**	Revelation 7 (Acts 15)

13 Sep. / 27 Elul
WEDNESDAY
DAY 28 OF REPENTANCE

14 Sep. / 28 Elul

THURSDAY

DAY 29 OF REPENTANCE

ROSH HASHANAH (FEAST OF TRUMPETS)

□ **TORAH** Genesis 21:22–27
□ **PROPHETS** Zephaniah 3
□ **WRITINGS** 2 Chronicles 23
□ **APOSTLES** Revelation 9:1–12 (Acts 16:19–40)

15 Sep. / 29 Elul
FRIDAY
ROSH HASHANAH EVE
DAY 30 OF REPENTANCE

CANDLE LIGHTING TIMES:

ROSH HASHANAH (FEAST OF TRUMPETS)

16 Sep. / 1 Tishrei

SHABBAT ●
ROSH HASHANAH 5784 DAY 1
(FEAST OF TRUMPETS)

DAY 31 OF REPENTANCE

Genesis 21:28–34   **TORAH** ☐
Numbers 28:11–15; 29:1–6
1 Samuel 1:1–2:10   **HAFTARAH** ☐
1 Thessalonians 4:13–18   **APOSTLES** ☐

CANDLE LIGHTING TIMES:

TODAY IN HISTORY: God creates Adam and Eve (tradition, Gen. 1:26f). "God created man in His own image, in the image of God He created him; male and female He created them." Waters of the Great Flood have drained, the dove does not return, and Noah removes the cover of the ark but remains inside (possible date, Gen. 8). "Now it came about in the six hundred and first year, in the first month [counting from Tishrei], on the first of the month, the water was dried up from the earth." Abraham binds his son Isaac to offer him on Mt. Moriah (tradition, Gen. 22). "Then they came to the place of which God had told him; and Abraham built the altar there and arranged the wood, and bound his son Isaac and laid him on the altar, on top of the wood." The daily sacrifice resumes (Ezr. 3:6). "From the first day of the seventh month they began to offer burnt offerings to the LORD, but the foundation of the temple of the LORD had not been laid." Ezra the Scribe reads the Torah to the people (Neh. 8:1f). "So on the first day of the seventh month Ezra the priest brought the Torah before the assembly" (NIV). Birth of Messiah in Bethlehem of Judah (possible date, Lk. 2). *Yamim Noraim* (Days of Awe) begin—the ten days from *Rosh HaShanah* to *Yom Kippur.*

ROSH HASHANAH (FEAST OF TRUMPETS)

□ TORAH   Genesis 22
           Numbers 28:11–15; 29:1–6
□ HAFTARAH   Jeremiah 31:2–20[1–19]
□ APOSTLES   1 Corinthians 15:35–58

17 Sep. / 2 Tishrei

● SUNDAY

ROSH HASHANAH 5784 DAY 2
(FEAST OF TRUMPETS)

DAY 32 OF REPENTANCE

TODAY IN HISTORY: The heads of families study Torah with Ezra (Neh. 8:13). "Then on the second day the heads of fathers' households of all the people, the priests and the Levites were gathered to Ezra the scribe that they might gain insight into the words of the Torah."

ROSH HASHANAH (FEAST OF TRUMPETS)

18 Sep. / 3 Tishrei

MONDAY
FAST OF GEDALIAH

DAY 33 OF REPENTANCE

Deuteronomy 32:1–6   **TORAH** ☐
Haggai 1–2   **PROPHETS** ☐
2 Chronicles 24   **WRITINGS** ☐
Revelation 9:13–21 (Acts 17)   **APOSTLES** ☐
SYNAGOGUE READINGS ☐
Exodus 32:11–14; 34:1–10; Isaiah 55:6–56:8 (afternoon)

TODAY IN HISTORY: The royal governor Gedaliah is murdered which marks the beginning of the end for the remnant in the Holy Land (tradition, 2 Ki. 25:25). "But it came about in the seventh month, that Ishmael the son of Nethaniah, the son of Elishama, of the royal family, came with ten men and struck Gedaliah down so that he died along with the Jews and the Chaldeans who were with him at Mizpah." The fast of the seventh month (Zec. 7:3f, 8:19). "The fast of the fourth, the fast of the fifth, the fast of the seventh and the fast of the tenth months will become joy, gladness, and cheerful feasts for the house of Judah." The Fast of Gedaliah is a shorter fast on the Jewish calendar and lasts from sunrise to sunset. It is one of four similar, biblical fast days. Normally observed on the 3rd of Tishrei, it may be moved if its observance would conflict with Shabbat.

HA'AZINU (LISTEN)

☐ **TORAH**	Deuteronomy 32:7–12	
☐ **PROPHETS**	Zechariah 1	
☐ **WRITINGS**	2 Chronicles 25	
☐ **APOSTLES**	Revelation 10 (Acts 18)	

19 Sep. / 4 Tishrei

TUESDAY

DAY 34 OF REPENTANCE

20 Sep. / 5 Tishrei

WEDNESDAY

DAY 35 OF REPENTANCE

Deuteronomy 32:13–18 **TORAH** ☐
Zechariah 2–3 **PROPHETS** ☐
2 Chronicles 26 **WRITINGS** ☐
Revelation 11 (Acts 19:1–20) **APOSTLES** ☐

HA'AZINU (LISTEN)

☐ **TORAH**	Deuteronomy 32:19–28
☐ **PROPHETS**	Zechariah 4–5
☐ **WRITINGS**	2 Chronicles 27
☐ **APOSTLES**	Revelation 12 (Acts 19:21–40)

21 Sep. / 6 Tishrei

THURSDAY
DAY 36 OF REPENTANCE

22 Sep. / 7 Tishrei

FRIDAY ◑

DAY 37 OF REPENTANCE

Deuteronomy 32:29–39 **TORAH** ☐
Zechariah 6–7 **PROPHETS** ☐
2 Chronicles 28 **WRITINGS** ☐
Revelation 13 (Acts 20) **APOSTLES** ☐

CANDLE LIGHTING TIMES:

HA'AZINU (LISTEN)

23 Sep. / 8 Tishrei

SHABBAT SHUVAH
(SABBATH OF RETURN)
DAY 38 OF REPENTANCE

TODAY IN HISTORY: *Shabbat Shuvah* (Sabbath of Return) is the Sabbath that occurs during the awe-filled days of trembling and repentance between *Rosh HaShanah* and *Yom Kippur*. The name *Shabbat Shuvah* comes from the first word of the prophetic portion that is read this Sabbath, Hosea 14:1–9[2–10]. "Return [*shuvah*], O Israel, to the LORD your God". *Shuvah* means "return" or "repent."   The 14-day dedication ceremony of the first Temple begins (1 Ki. 8). "All the men of Israel assembled themselves to King Solomon at the feast, in the month Ethanim, which is the seventh month."   The circumcision of Messiah (possible date, Lk. 2:21).

HA'AZINU (LISTEN)

24 Sep. / 9 Tishrei

SUNDAY
YOM KIPPUR EVE

DAY 39 OF REPENTANCE

Leviticus 22:26–33 **TORAH** ☐
Zechariah 8 **PROPHETS** ☐
2 Chronicles 29:1–19 **WRITINGS** ☐
Revelation 14 (Acts 21:1–19) **APOSTLES** ☐

CANDLE LIGHTING TIMES:

YOM KIPPUR (DAY OF ATONEMENT)

SYNAGOGUE READINGS
- ☐ Leviticus 16 (morning)
- ☐ Numbers 29:7–11 (morning)
- ☐ Isaiah 57:14–58:14 (morning)
- ☐ James 4:1–12 (Messianic, morning)
- ☐ Leviticus 18 (afternoon)
- ☐ **Book of Jonah 1–4** (afternoon)
- ☐ Micah 7:18–20 (afternoon)
- ☐ 2 Peter 3:9–14 (Messianic, afternoon)

25 Sep. / 10 Tishrei

MONDAY
YOM KIPPUR
(DAY OF ATONEMENT)

TODAY IN HISTORY: New stone tablets are given (tradition, Ex. 34:28–29). "When Moses came down from Mount Sinai with the two tablets of the Testimony in his hands, he was not aware that his face was radiant because he had spoken with the LORD" (NIV). Messiah discusses the driving out of demons, blasphemy, and the sign of Jonah (possible date, Mt. 12:22f). "Therefore I say to you, any sin and blasphemy shall be forgiven people, but blasphemy against the Spirit shall not be forgiven."

YOM KIPPUR (DAY OF ATONEMENT)

26 Sep. / 11 Tishrei
TUESDAY

Leviticus 23:1–3 **TORAH** ☐
Zechariah 9 **PROPHETS** ☐
2 Chronicles 29:20–36 **WRITINGS** ☐
Revelation 15 (Acts 21:20–40) **APOSTLES** ☐

SUKKOT (TABERNACLES)

☐ **TORAH**   Leviticus 23:4–8
☐ **PROPHETS**   Zechariah 10
☐ **WRITINGS**   2 Chronicles 30
☐ **APOSTLES**   Revelation 16 (Acts 22)

27 Sep. / 12 Tishrei
WEDNESDAY

SUKKOT (TABERNACLES)

28 Sep. / 13 Tishrei
THURSDAY

Leviticus 23:9–14 **TORAH** ☐
Zechariah 11 **PROPHETS** ☐
2 Chronicles 31 **WRITINGS** ☐
Revelation 17 (Acts 23) **APOSTLES** ☐

SUKKOT (TABERNACLES)

☐ **TORAH** Leviticus 23:15–22
☐ **PROPHETS** Zechariah 12
☐ **WRITINGS** 2 Chronicles 32
☐ **APOSTLES** Revelation 18:1–13 (Acts 24)

29 Sep. / 14 Tishrei

○ FRIDAY
SUKKOT EVE

CANDLE LIGHTING TIMES:

SUKKOT (TABERNACLES)

30 Sep. / 15 Tishrei

SHABBAT
SUKKOT DAY 1 (TABERNACLES)

Leviticus 23:23–44   **TORAH** ☐
Numbers 29:12–16
Zechariah 14   **HAFTARAH** ☐
Revelation 7:9–17   **APOSTLES** ☐

CANDLE LIGHTING TIMES:

SUKKOT (TABERNACLES)

1 Oct. / 16 Tishrei
SUNDAY
OUTSIDE ISRAEL: **SUKKOT DAY 2***
(TABERNACLES)

* It is customary among the Jewish people, since ancient times, to double the festival sabbath (*yom tov*) outside Israel.

2 Oct. / 17 Tishrei

MONDAY
SUKKOT DAY 3 (TABERNACLES)

Deuteronomy 14:22–29   **TORAH** ☐
Numbers 29:17–22
Zechariah 13   **PROPHETS** ☐
2 Chronicles 33   **WRITINGS** ☐
Revelation 18:14–24 (Acts 25)   **APOSTLES** ☐

☐ **TORAH**	Deuteronomy 15:1–18
	Numbers 29:20–25
☐ **PROPHETS**	Zechariah 14
☐ **WRITINGS**	2 Chronicles 34:1–17
☐ **APOSTLES**	Revelation 19 (Acts 26)

3 Oct. / 18 Tishrei
TUESDAY
SUKKOT DAY 4 (TABERNACLES)

TODAY IN HISTORY: Messiah begins to teach in the Temple during *Sukkot* (possible date, Jn. 7:14). "But when it was now the midst of the feast Yeshua went up into the temple, and began to teach."

4 Oct. / 19 Tishrei
WEDNESDAY
SUKKOT DAY 5 (TABERNACLES)

Deuteronomy 15:19–23 **TORAH** ☐
Numbers 29:23–28
Malachi 1 **PROPHETS** ☐
2 Chronicles 34:18–33 **WRITINGS** ☐
Revelation 20 (Acts 27:1–20) **APOSTLES** ☐

5 Oct. / 20 Tishrei
THURSDAY
SUKKOT DAY 6 (TABERNACLES)

6 Oct. / 21 Tishrei

FRIDAY ◑

SUKKOT DAY 7 / HOSHANA RABBA
(TABERNACLES / GREAT HOSANNA)

Deuteronomy 16:4–8   **TORAH** ☐
Numbers 29:26–34
Malachi 3–4   **PROPHETS** ☐
2 Chronicles 36   **WRITINGS** ☐
Revelation 22 (Acts 28)   **APOSTLES** ☐

CANDLE LIGHTING TIMES: _____

TODAY IN HISTORY: Haggai prophesies about the glory of the Second Temple (Hag. 2:2f). "On the twenty-first of the seventh month, the word of the LORD came by Haggai the prophet." Messiah speaks of the living water of the Spirit on the day for the water ceremony in the Temple (Jn. 7:37–39). "Now on the last day, the great day of the feast, Yeshua stood and cried out, saying, 'If anyone is thirsty, let him come to Me and drink.'" Death of Messianic pioneer Rabbi Isaac Lichtenstein (zt"l) year 5669 (1908 CE). Isaac Lichtenstain was a Hungarian Orthodox rabbi who became a believer in Yeshua as Messiah, yet did not renounce Judaism nor his post as district rabbi. He wrote several pamphlets arguing that faith in Yeshua is compatible with Judaism. Eventually community pressure forced him out of his position as district rabbi, but he refused to give up his Jewish identity (vineofdavid.org).

SUKKOT (TABERNACLES)

☐ **TORAH**	Deuteronomy 16:9–17	
	Numbers 29:35–40[30:1]	
☐ **HAFTARAH**	1 Kings 8:54–9:1[8:66]	
☐ **WRITINGS**	**Book of Ecclesiastes 1–12**	
☐ **APOSTLES**	John 7:53–8:12	

7 Oct. / 22 Tishrei
SHABBAT
SHMINI ATZERET (EIGHTH DAY)

CANDLE LIGHTING TIMES:

TODAY IN HISTORY: Messiah disqualifies the witnesses against a woman caught in adultery (possible date if the placement of Jn. 7:53–8:11 is correct). "Early in the morning He came again into the temple, and all the people were coming to Him…"

SUKKOT (TABERNACLES)

8 Oct. / 23 Tishrei

SUNDAY
OUTSIDE ISRAEL: **SIMCHAT TORAH***
(REJOICING OF THE TORAH)

Deuteronomy 33:1–34:12	**TORAH** ☐
Genesis 1:1–2:3	
Numbers 29:35–40[30:1]	
Joshua 1	**PROPHETS** ☐
Psalm 1	**WRITINGS** ☐
Matthew 1 (James 1)	**APOSTLES** ☐

TODAY IN HISTORY: King Solomon sends the people home after a 14-day celebration. "Then on the twenty-third day of the seventh month he sent the people to their tents, rejoicing and happy of heart because of the goodness that the LORD had shown to David and to Solomon and to His people Israel" (2 Chr. 7:10). * It is customary among the Jewish people, since ancient times, to double the festival sabbath (*yom tov*) outside Israel.

BERESHEET (IN THE BEGINNING)

⁓Happy Simchat Torah⁓

CONGRATULATIONS! It is a great joy and strenght to read through the Bible in one year together! We hope your daily walk with the Lord has been strengthened. By God's grace, the new edition of *Daily Bread* is now available from Ariel Media (*arielmedia.shop*). In case you do not yet have a copy, an additional month of references are available below:

9 OCT. / 24 TISHREI
Genesis 2:4–19
Joshua 2
Psalm 2
Matthew 2 (Jas 2)

10 OCT. / 25 TISHREI
Genesis 2:20–3:21
Joshua 3–4
Psalm 3–4
Matthew 3 (Jas 3)

11 OCT. / 26 TISHREI
Genesis 3:22–4:18
Joshua 5
Psalm 5
Matthew 4 (Jas 4)

12 OCT. / 27 TISHREI
Genesis 4:19–22
Joshua 6
Psalm 6
Matthew 5:1–26 (Jas 5)

13 OCT. / 28 TISHREI
Genesis 4:23–5:24
Joshua 7
Psalm 7
Matthew 5:27–48 (1 Pet 1)

14 OCT. / 29 TISHREI
SHABBAT BERESHEET
Genesis 5:25–6:8
1 Samuel 20:18–42
Revelation 21:9–27

15 OCT. / 30 TISHREI
Genesis 6:9–22
Numbers 28:11–15
Joshua 8
Psalm 8
Matthew 6 (1 Pet 2)

16 OCT. / 1 CHESHVAN
Genesis 7:1–16
Numbers 28:11–15
Joshua 9
Psalm 9
Matthew 7 (1 Pet 3)

17 OCT. / 2 CHESHVAN
Genesis 7:17–8:14
Joshua 10
Psalm 10
Matthew 8 (1 Pet 4)

18 OCT. / 3 CHESHVAN
Genesis 8:15–9:7
Joshua 11
Psalm 11
Matthew 9 (1 Pet 5)

19 OCT. / 4 CHESHVAN
Genesis 9:8–17
Joshua 12
Psalm 12
Matthew 10 (2 Pet 1)

20 OCT. / 5 CHESHVAN
Genesis 9:18–10:32
Joshua 13
Psalm 13
Matthew 11 (2 Pet 2)

21 OCT. / 6 CHESHVAN
SHABBAT NOACH
Genesis 11:1–32
Isaiah 54:1–55:5
2 Peter 3:1–14

22 OCT. / 7 CHESHVAN
Genesis 12:1–13
Joshua 14
Psalm 14
Matthew 12:1–21 (2 Pet 3)

23 OCT. / 8 CHESHVAN
Genesis 12:14–13:4
Joshua 15
Psalm 15
Matthew 12:22–50 (1 Jn 1)

24 OCT. / 9 CHESHVAN
Genesis 13:5–18
Joshua 16–17
Psalm 16
Matthew 13:1–30 (1 Jn 2)

25 OCT. / 10 CHESHVAN
Genesis 14:1–20
Joshua 18
Psalm 17
Matthew 13:31–58 (1 Jn 3)

26 OCT. / 11 CHESHVAN
Genesis 14:21–15:6
Joshua 19
Psalm 18
Matthew 14 (1 Jn 4)

27 OCT. / 12 CHESHVAN
Genesis 15:7–17:6
Joshua 20
Psalm 19
Matthew 15 (1 Jn 5)

28 OCT. / 13 CHESHVAN
SHABBAT LECH LECHA
Genesis 17:7–27
Isaiah 40:27–41:16
Romans 4:1–12

29 OCT. / 14 CHESHVAN
Genesis 18:1–14
Joshua 21
Psalm 20
Matthew 16 (2 Jn)

30 OCT. / 15 CHESHVAN
Genesis 18:15–33
Joshua 22
Psalm 21
Matthew 17 (3 Jn)

31 OCT. / 16 CHESHVAN
Genesis 19:1–20
Joshua 23
Psalm 22
Matthew 18 (Jude)

1 NOV. / 17 CHESHVAN
Genesis 19:21–21:4
Joshua 24
Psalm 23
Matthew 19 (Ro 1)

2 NOV. / 18 CHESHVAN
Genesis 21:5–21
Judges 1
Psalm 24
Matthew 20 (Ro 2)

3 NOV. / 19 CHESHVAN
Genesis 21:22–34
Judges 2
Psalm 25
Matthew 21:1–22 (Ro 3)

4 NOV. / 20 CHESHVAN
SHABBAT VAYERA
Genesis 22:1–24
2 Kings 4:1–37
Hebrews 11:8–19

5 NOV. / 21 CHESHVAN
Genesis 23:1–16
Judges 3
Psalm 26
Matthew 21:23–46 (Ro 4)

6 NOV. / 22 CHESHVAN
Genesis 23:17–24:9
Judges 4
Psalm 27
Matthew 22:1–22 (Ro 5)

7 NOV. / 23 CHESHVAN
Genesis 24:10–26
Judges 5
Psalm 28
Matthew 22:23–46 (Ro 6)

8 NOV. / 24 CHESHVAN
Genesis 24:27–52
Judges 6
Psalm 29
Matthew 23 (Ro 7)

9 NOV. / 25 CHESHVAN
Genesis 24:53–67
Judges 7
Psalm 30
Matthew 24:1-28 (Ro 8:1-17)

*weekly*TORAH

BIBLE COMMENTARIES BY LARS ENARSON

Do you want to dig deeper into what you are reading? Each week, Lars Enarson, the lead creator of Daily Bread, has written a commentary on the weekly Torah portion, focused on practical discipleship to Messiah. In one year, get a thorough foundation in that part of the Bible that many know very little about, yet which makes up the foundation for all Scriptural revelation. Available on video and in print.

SIGN UP FOR WEEKLY TORAH AT
THEWATCHMAN.ORG

Daily Bread

FOR BUSY
MOMS

Ladies, check out *Daily Bread for Busy Moms*, a daily Bible-reading podcast from Israel! Connect with the vibrant community on Instagram, iTunes, and SoundCloud. To subscribe, go to:

DAILYBREADMOMS.COM

Endnotes

Rosh Chodesh means 'New Moon'. *Shabbat* means 'Sabbath'. *Haftarah* refers to the prophetic text read after the Torah.

Note: The enumeration of some verses differ between English and Hebrew published Bibles. DAILY BREAD gives the verse references found in most English translations and the corresponding Hebrew verses within brackets [ ]. The blessings after the "Introduction" are from the traditional Jewish prayer book and also adapted from the *Complete Jewish Bible.* The calendar and historical information is based on research and the sources below. The traditional synagogue readings follow the Ashkenazi tradition. The Messianic readings for Sabbaths and holidays are suggestions and do not follow an established tradition.

SOURCES

Artscroll Series: Chumash Stone Edition Travel Size (Ashkenaz), Nosson Scherman (Brooklyn, NY: Mesorah Publications Ltd. 1998).

Chabad.org/calendar (2013/8/15).

Complete Jewish Bible, copyright © 1998 by David H. Stern (Clarksville, MD/Jerusalem, Israel: Jewish New Testament Publications, Inc. 1998).

Eretz Yisrael Land of Israel 5772/2011–2012 Calendar (Marshfield, MO: First Fruits of Zion, 2011. www.ffoz.org).

Hebcal.com (2016–2022).

Vineofdavid.org (2012/9/13).